Christian Unschooling

Growing Your Children *in the* Freedom *of* Christ

Christian Unschooling

Growing Your Children *in the* Freedom *of* Christ

By Teri J Brown
with Elissa M Wahl

CHAMPION PRESS, LTD.

CHAMPION PRESS, LTD.
VANCOUVER, WASHINGTON

ISBN 1-891400-22-3
LCCN 2001086217

Manufactured in Canada 10 9 8 7 6 5 4 3 2 1

Acknowledgements

Teri...

I give thanks to Christ, my Savior, without whom I would be a mess. Big thanks and hugs to my husband, my "Mon" for his support even when the house became a bit messy at times. Huge thanks to my children who loved even the back of Mom's head. Brook, thanks for taking a chance. My friends ... Linda, see you in the office. Beth, keep cheering, it's a gift. Thank you, Kim ... keep the red pen ... you know I need it! Tammie, my sister, "Go Aussie!" Debi ... I have learned so much from you. Teraisa ... thanks for believing in me. Great research, Elissa, if it's out there you will find it!

But mostly I dedicate this book to Mildred Wall. Grandma, I am writing because of you.

Elissa...

God needs praise foremost, then my parents for instilling in me the beliefs I have, my husband for supporting me, my children for showing me angels really can be here on earth and Jeanne for being my sounding board all the time. Teri, thanks for being such a great partner! I already mentioned God, but He really deserves all the credit, without Him, none of this would have fallen into place.

Contents

PART TWO: THE ESSAYS

Introduction

It's amazing how many books have been started with a conversation. This book is no exception. Elissa and I were "talking" online, about being a Christian and an unschooler and how isolating that felt at times. I was telling her I felt estranged from my Christian homeschooling friends because of my educational philosophies and isolated from many of my unschooling peers because of my faith. She told me that she had felt the same way, but was realizing that there were many more Christian unschoolers out there than she had previously thought. In that conversation a seed was planted in both our minds.

After much prayer and thought, that seed germinated and flourished and a book was born. We were quite sure this book was to be a collection of essays by Christians of faith who were unschooling. Neither of us wanted to set ourselves up as unschooling experts. The very nature of unschooling isn't a formulaic approach, but rather a highly individualized endeavor. Unschooling for one family is quite different than the unschooling in another family. By following your child's interests and God given gifts, you will be heading down a very different road than other Christian unschoolers.

Before beginning the book, we wished to have a few concrete goals in mind. Our main goals fell into three categories:

- To support Christian unschoolers and let them know they are not alone.
- To give hope and information to those Christian parents who are burning out from a strict "school at home" schedule and to inform them of another option.
- To let Christian homeschoolers everywhere know that not only do Christian unschoolers exist, but we are growing in numbers and we do not believe our methods are less righteous or unbiblical than those of curriculum using homeschoolers.

We felt that giving unschooling Christians a voice was the best way to obtain those goals.

This book is also unique in that while writing it, Elissa and I never met and rarely spoke on the phone. The Internet was our main method of communication. We passed ideas and chapters back and forth as easily as if we were in the same office. Living on opposite sides of the United States, our chances of meeting in person were slim and long distance rates prevented us from calling one another except for the most exciting of news and generally even that was limited to "You have to get online! Big Stuff!" In spite of these hindrances we got to know one another well, we shared joys and heartaches, prayed for each other and encouraged each other, and always, always kept the Lord upper most in our minds while we worked.

We put out the call for contributors everywhere. We wrote articles about the book for support group newsletters and magazines alike. Then we sat back and waited. We didn't have to wait long, the essays came pouring in. From our mail boxes and across the phone lines, Christian unschoolers were sharing their stories. They shared with us their hopes, dreams, accomplishments and activities. The essays were so different, yet had so much in common, their desire to allow God to work in their children unencumbered by their own agendas.

It is our hope that this book and their stories will uplift and encourage you in your efforts. Unschooling isn't something that is unbiblical, nor anti-educational, but a wonderful way to allow our Lord the freedom to work in a child's life.

Chapter One

What is Unschooling?

The Dream

Ahhhhh, the homeschooling dream. How many of us held a preconceived notion of homeschooling in our minds when we first decided to educate our children at home? When most people think of homeschooling, they picture a loving mother bending over a table lined with bright and shiny children. Breakfast dishes are nowhere in sight and morning devotions have been done. The mother is patient, loving, kind and tireless in her efforts of raising her children. The children are well-mannered and obedient, eager to learn the pearls of wisdom falling from their mother's mouth.

The Reality

A mother, still in her robe, is trying to wipe the table free of crumbs while a sick toddler whines while clinging to her legs. After several false starts she finally gets all the children to the table which is still sticky with jam. Her six-year-old is clutching his paper airplanes, making loud whirring noises while flying reconnaissance missions over the juice his three-year-old sister has just spilled. After cleaning the juice she distracts the two youngest with a story tape then sets her eight-year-old with the poem he was supposed to copy last Monday. According to her teacher planning book, the one falling apart from frequent erasing, they are one week behind. She sighs when she notices that her eight-year-old is tapping his pencil and staring out the window with a vacant look in his eyes.

She reprimands him and they begin their tri-weekly fight over school work. She is demanding and cajoling and he is both defiant and defeated until they are both in tears and she sends him to his room. Her six-year-old looks up at her, "Do I have to do my handwriting," he asks. Tired of arguing she shakes her head no and he happily scampers off to play with his airplanes. "Lord," she asks silently, "why is this so hard? I was so sure that you wanted me to homeschool my children. They are so obedient in so many things, why is our school such a struggle?" Feeling like a failure she wonders if they wouldn't be better off in a public or private school.

This book will show you how to escape homeschool burnout and the push and pull trap through the method of unschooling. We will also clear up many of the misconceptions Christians have about unschooling. The unschooling method offers parents and children an educational alternative that is healthy, effective and a joy to the entire family.

The Possibilities

(same family three months later)

The mother sits on the floor playing Candyland with her two youngest children while her six-year-old lays next to her carefully copying a picture of an F 15 Eagle out of an encyclopedia. He has quite a collection of airplane drawings now and has even shown an interest in learning to read the books on flight that he borrowed from the library. The game finished, she pulls a chair up to the counter and shows her three-year-old how to make juice, counting out the cans of water together and showing her where the two quart line is on the pitcher. While doing this, her eight year old bursts in the door, bringing with him the freshness of the outdoors, where he has been playing for the last hour. "Look what I found, Mom!" he cries as he excitedly shows her the tiny salamander in the palm of his hand. "I'm going to put it my terrarium." He takes the lid off the terrarium that he had carefully constructed after much research. It already housed several snails and a slug.

"You better find out what it eats, Bud," the mother reminds him. "I know." He says grinning at her and crossing the room to the computer, "I'll look it up on Encarta."

Unschooling, child-led learning, free learning, interest based education, child delighted learning. These are all terms for what this book is about. But what do they mean exactly? Good question. The best way to answer that is to first explore what unschooling doesn't mean.

What Unschooling Doesn't Mean

- Unschooling does not mean raising your children without discipline.
- Unschooling does not mean allowing your children to do nothing all day except watch television and play video games.
- Unschooling does not mean you are too lazy to teach your children the "proper way."
- Unschooling does not mean anti-Christian. True, there are unschoolers who are Jewish, Muslim, Buddhists, agnostics, etc. However, we are Christians and we are unschoolers and that is what this book is all about.

To me, unschooling means raising your children in the freedom of Christ. To allow the Lord to show us the gifts he has given them and the freedom to develop those gifts to the fullest. It means the faith to let God show your children what they should learn and to trust them to learn it. It means letting their God given curiosity lead them in the exciting quest of exploring the world around them. It means... I could go on and on.

Different Meanings for Different Families

If the truth be told, unschooling means different things to different people. A better way to ask that question would be, "What does unschooling mean to you?" Which is how we phrased the question when we took our informal unschooling survey. The answers to that question are as unique as the people answering it. I am including them here in order to give you an idea of how complex the question actually is.

"Unschooling is a process by which we change our own ideas of learning. Most of us were taught in a classroom. Thus, in allowing our children to lead the learning process, we are constantly learning ourselves. I guess to me it is the entire lifelong process of living, loving and learning in our natural home environment." Leslie Theurer, Missouri

"Helping your children learn how to teach themselves. Being a facilitator, question answerer, resource giver, but not always a teacher." Lynne L. Henderson, Washington

"Unschooling means to me, using whatever works for each child to fulfill their potential. It is not separating learning from life, but embracing learning, through everyday activities. It is not following a scope-and-sequence developed by professionals, but using teachable moments to teach our children what they need—when they need it" Michele Hastings, Canada

"I define unschooling as a lifestyle of learning. Learning through life not only from a pre-planned curriculum. Letting each child pursue his or her God-given talents and desires." Kathleen Smith, California

"Child led learning with a push every now and again. Learning without time or space boundaries. Learning with love." Alice Steen, Georgia

"No workbooks, no textbooks forced upon the child. We have some curriculum, but our policy, effective immediately, is that the child has to ask to do the books. Then I will gladly sit down with them and help them do a page or two or three or whatever the child requests." Jeanne Musfeldt, Iowa

"I have a definite set of goals in mind for my kids to know/learn during their homeschooling .They need to be able to read well, write well and do math. Every-

thing else can be pursued to their heart's content. They spend days obsessed with a project. It doesn't matter, there is no hurry. I don't believe in coercing them to learn. When you force knowledge upon someone, they only memorize it. They don't understand it on a deeper level, and they don't see how it fits into other pieces of the world. Unschooling is a way of letting them discover the 'big picture."
Susan Viator, Oregon

Complicated is right. With so many definitions of unschooling floating around how do you know which one is the right one? Basically, they all are. All of these definitions carry a common theme that can give you a clue to the real heart of Christian unschooling.

" I guess to me it is the entire lifelong process of living, loving and learning in our natural home environment."

"Helping your children learn how to teach themselves."

"Unschooling, to me, is allowing the children to decide what things they are interested in and what they want to learn about."

"I define unschooling as Child-directed learning."

The common theme is allowing your children the freedom to choose, in most cases, what they will learn. Unschooling involves allowing the Lord the freedom to work within each child. Whether you are completely unstructured in your learning environment or offer periodic guidance, children who are unschooled have more individual freedom and empowerment when it comes to their education than their homeschooled contemporaries.

Chapter Two

Why Unschooling?

Why does unschooling or interest-initiated learning work? Why did we feel it such an effective method that we would devote an entire book to it, along with the countless families who took the time to write essays on the subject? What is it about unschooling that makes it, in our opinion, one of the most effective ways to educate your children?

The Lord Made Us Unique

For you formed my inward parts; You covered me in my mother's womb. I will praise. You, for I am fearfully and wonderfully made. Marvelous are your works, And that my soul knows very well. Psalms. 139: 13, 14

The Lord created us to be unique on the face of the earth. We have a large portion of our brain that is empty, so to speak, waiting for input. Unlike animals, we are not filled with instinctive behaviors. Thomas Armstrong, Ph.D. puts it this way in his book, *Awakening your Child's Natural Genius*, "Endowed at birth with large portions of the brain uncommitted to any set plan or behavior, the child grows up as a natural learner, capable of responding to the changing demands and currents of life with remarkable flexibility."

Think about just how much we learn and retain in our first five years of life. Speaking, walking, learning to brush our teeth, eating with a fork... all of these things are behaviors learned from those around us. Even the motivation for potty training is less an exercise in training than an attempt to mimic and please others. The Lord made us adaptive and innovative. He knew us when we were in the womb, and gifted each of us with a uniqueness unlike anything else in his creation.

Please note, that while we believe that all children are gifted, do not misinterpret that to mean that all children are born good. We are all born in sin, not born "bad" mind you, but with the capabilities for wrong or evil doing. The Lord says that none are righteous, and we believe that. But we are also capable of great good, how could we not be, made in the image of our creator, who defines good. Children are gifted because the Lord made them all unique, with strengths and weaknesses. If children are all different, created to be their own special person by our Lord who fashioned us, would it not stand to reason that all children learn differently and have different learning needs? That we should seek his will in our dealings with our children and trust in him to help us to raise and teach them?

Unschooling or interest initiated learning, works because it takes into account all the things that God created us to be.

How Children Learn

"Assuredly, I say to you, unless you are converted and come to me as a little child, you will by no means enter the kingdom of heaven." Matthew 18:3

How do children come to the Lord? They come with faith and humility. How do children go about learning? They learn by the faith that they will find the answers to their never-ending stream of questions. They come with the humility that they know very little about this vast world. The world is amazing to a young child, but it is by no means unknowable. Children make wondrous discoveries every day.

The Environment Factor

The environment your children live in affects their learning. Children are able to learn in a negative environment, but rarely thrive. In order for unschooling to work to its fullest potential, an educational environment must be created. Mom and Dad must have books readily available and must be seen reading. Math must be shown as a valuable subject that is used in every day life. Parents must have interests, passions and an eagerness to learn. Values are caught, and if a child observes learning as a precious gift from God, that is the way he will approach it as well.

Children must be nurtured as a whole. This means not compartmentalizing the child's life into different groups like religious instruction, socialization, character development, education, etc. For the Christian unschooler, all of these different aspects of life come under one heading, LIFE. Teaching our children about God is something that permeates everyday life. Learning socialization comes from living together daily. Education comes from leading a life rich in curiosity and searching for the answers to our questions.

Can Christians Be Unschoolers?

To a small segment of Christians, Christian unschooling is an oxymoron. This school of thought has dangerous connotations for Christians who are unschoolers. It can also make Christian unschooling a very lonely business. We are often shunned by our fellow Christians for our educational philosophies, even told that we cannot be good Christians if we are unschoolers.

I have seen Christian based websites devoted solely to pointing out to Christian unschoolers the error of our unschooling ways. Perhaps one of the chief problems lie in the unschooling definition of teaching and training by example and nurturing, compared to the structured and regimented definition of teaching and training.

Many of these assumptions are based on a faulty perception of what unschooling is. It is a fallacy, I feel, to think unschooling is *only* child led learning. Most of the unschooling parents we know, attempt to put learning experiences in the child's path. Not forced learning, mind you, but real life experiences. For example, it's important to my husband and

I, that our children have a working knowledge of consumer math before they leave the home. One of the things we have recently begun to do is give them a certain amount of money to buy a week's worth of lunches. This is a real world way to learn real world skills.

Here are some of the reasons critics feel that Christians can't be unschoolers.

Original Sin

Many Christians who are opposed to unschooling believe that because we are born with a sin nature, children must therefore be lazy and unwilling to learn. We challenge that assumption.

As Christians, we do believe in sin nature, but that does not mean we believe that evil is the only fruit that humans can produce. The Bible says that we are created in the image of God. Does that not mean that we are also capable of good and beauty? Both Christians and non Christians have done great good and created works of great beauty. Because of our sin nature both Christians and non Christians have committed unspeakable evil. Being born in sin does not mean being born "bad." It means that we have a tendency towards selfish or self-centered behavior. It also means that we are born separate from God.

A God Of Order

"What about the fact that our Lord is a God of order? He wouldn't want us learning things in a disorderly way." This argument is often offered from those Christians who do not believe in unschooling. I agree, The Lord is a God of order. His order, not ours. His timing, not ours. Who better than the Lord to direct the learning of our children? He knows them and His Will for their lives far better then we ever can.

When one of my children shows an interest in a subject, he will often, quite naturally, study it in a basic order. Children reach out and grasp concepts that are easily understandable for their own stage of development. When asked to teach something, I endeavor to teach in the same way.

Teaching Diligently

You shall teach them diligently to your children, and shall talk of them when they sit in your house, when you walk by the way, when you lie down, and when you rise up. Deuteronomy 6:7

The Lord clearly gives parents the responsibility of raising our children in the nurture and admonishment of the Lord. The Bible is not clear, however, on the exact methods of how we are to go about that. It states we are to be diligent. I try to be diligent in the example I present. We are diligent in our attendance of church. It also states that we are to teach them. Most unschoolers do teach their children, we teach them daily. We teach them to tie their shoes, make a batch of brownies and comparison shop, among other things.

We are diligent in finding mentors for them, in searching out creative ways to satisfy their curiosity, in being there for them every day to facilitate their learning. This is another fallacy, that unschoolers are not involved in their children's education. In reality, unschoolers are among the most diligent people I have met.

Jesus As Our Model

In most of the arguments against Christian unschooling, are numerous examples about the edicts of the Lord to train our children in the admonishment of the Lord. Almost every single Bible verse, I have seen, on this subject, pertains to teaching our children about the Lord and his ways. Teach our children diligently of the Lord. As a Christian, I am to look to Christ for my example. How did he teach?

The students closest to Christ were the 12 disciples. They followed Him, ate with Him, worked with Him and listened to Him. They LIVED with him, following his example.

Why should I choose packets or curriculum to teach my children when Christ did not have one for His disciples? How can we please God today with our actions? What gifts has the Lord given to my children that he wants them to develop? What interests has He put in my children's hearts that He wants us to learn about? That is what we need to know.

I believe the Lord has a plan for my children's lives, it is my job to do whatever I can to help them discover that plan. Wouldn't overbearing meddling with curriculum or scope and sequence, merely put obstructions in His way? My own agenda is not the point in following the Lord—finding HIS will for our lives is.

Christians can be unschoolers, in fact, unschooling is one of the best ways I've found for allowing the Lord to develop in my children the wonderful gifts He gave them.

Chapter Three

Getting Started

Going from a structured atmosphere to one that is less so can be a nerve wracking process. The decision to unschool your children is one that takes prayer, research and faith. Once you've made that choice the next question is, inevitably, "How do I start?" So many people have started out with a "school at home" philosophy, I've decided to devote an entire chapter to relaxing your homeschool into an unschool. This chapter will give you hints and encouragement for embarking on your new adventure.

Age

I'm often asked the question, "What is the best age to begin unschooling your children?" The answer is simple, the best age to begin unschooling your children is whatever age they're at right now. Unschooling is a term and method that can begin at birth, after several years of school or even in the teenage years. I started unschooling myself as an adult and have learned more the past few years than in my entire school career.

Often people make the mistake of thinking that teens need to crack down and study and that unschooling isn't practical for a youth looking to go to college. Not so. Teenagers who are unschooled often make excellent students as they have much experience in knowing how to learn.

Deschooling Vs. Starting Right In

Many people subscribe to the deschooling theory. Deschooling is generally used in cases where a child is being pulled from a private or public school to go into a homeschool environment. It is a term used to describe the transition time between when a child leaves the school, until their love of learning returns. A loose rule of thumb would be, for every year the child spent in school, a month of deschooling would be needed. Any child going from a structured school atmosphere, to an unstructured one, needs some quiet, down time. Parents are going to need this transition time as well…use it to get to know your children's unique learning style.

I know when I made the switch from a more structured atmosphere to an unstructured one, it was very helpful to take a couple of weeks off to get used to the feel of freedom again. My children were not accustomed to having so many educational choices and it took them a while to want to "study" anything. Once freed from the constraints of a structured atmosphere, they were ready to relax all day. I casually offered fun trips and projects. Soon both were ready for more "solid" activities.

I've chosen to list a few ideas which have proven to be invaluable to unschooling in my family. Feel free to use these or adapt them to fit the needs of your family.

Journaling

After two weeks of "vacation" for both my children and I, I began to keep a journal of their daily activities. This was both an exercise in curiosity and a pacifier for my very structured husband who, although supportive of our decision to unschool, was still rather nervous. I was delighted by the results of my journaling and would highly recommend it for anyone who is unsure of their unschooling decision. It's very reassuring. Part of a typical day would look like this:

Ethan: Played for an hour with Lego's building planes, looked up planes in Encyclopedia (reading, science, research skills, spatial reasoning). Played outside, watched anthill and looked for queen (science, observation). Worked for another hour building playhouse with his sister (measuring, cooperation, problem solving). Went to grocery store with me and helped find best bargains (math, home-ec.). Watched *The Magic School Bus* (science). Listened to me read *Little House in the Big Woods* (listening skills, literature, history).

Megan: Played piano for 20 minutes (music). Wrote a song (music and writing). Built playhouse with her brother (measuring, cooperation, problem solving). Went to a friend's house and made chocolate chip cookies (socialization, math, home-ec.). Spent an hour outside drawing birds in her nature notebook (art, observation, science). Listened to me read Little House on the Big Woods (listening skills, literature, history).

After several weeks of this, my husband and I were reassured enough to give journaling up, they were learning all the time and besides, I was tired of trying to write down everything they did in a day!

Bridging the Gap Between Structure and Unschooling

Many people use literature as a stepping stone toward unschooling. The library is the perfect place to start doing this. Allow your children to get their own library cards, then let them browse for books. I'm fairly lenient in which books they choose as far as difficulty goes, though I am a bit more picky concerning subject matter. I have seen my children choose nonfiction books I felt were above their reading level only to find them completely absorbed by them. They might not finish the whole book, but they get what they need. You might be surprised at the depth of their choices. Books your children choose are far more liable to be read.

We love to read aloud and the variety of topics we cover this way is astonishing. Last year we read both classics and modern works, poetry, fiction and nonfiction. We covered history from pre-revolutionary war, *The Witch of Blackbird Pond* and *The Sign of the Beaver* to the Civil War, *Little Women.* We read poetry as diverse as Shel Silverstein, Walt Whitman and Emily Dickinson. It's very likely a first rate education can be obtained by reading alone.

Unit Studies

I have noticed unit studies are another common bridge between structured learning and non structured learning. Have your children make a list of things they're interested in. Take one item and help them research it. There are so many resources at your local library, one subject can easily turn into a mini unit study. One example is to try this with a country. You can touch on the literature, culture, language and food of the country, to name just a few. This method gives your children the opportunity to practice making their own educational choices, while reassuring you that they're doing something. My children made such a list and I was astonished at the variety of their choices. At what other school can you learn about pigs, France, sign language, cars and cooking? You also might want to choose one subject to study as a family. It's much easier coming up with ideas for one unit study at a time than trying to come up with activities for several different topics. Once your children do several unit studies they will begin to learn how to approach learning in diverse ways and to look at topics with an eye for the unusual.

The Charlotte Mason Method

As any Charlotte Mason purist will be sure to tell you, Charlotte Mason, did advocate a schedule. However, many of her techniques are so child friendly that they lend themselves wonderfully to the unschooling method. For those who are wanting to relax their homeschools into an unschool, but who are reluctant to make such a leap, some of the Charlotte Mason Methods might be just right for you. Our children still work in their nature notebooks and narration is now a part of our normal daily life. Narration is the "telling back" of information processed and one of the cornerstones of the Charlotte Mason method most easily utilized as children love to tell of what they have seen or read.

When Are You Ready for the Final Step into Unschooling?

Some people continue to utilize these different methods clear through their children's educations, while others make a complete break with educational structure into unschooling. Incorporating unit studies or narration into your unschool is as simple as incorporating such activities into your life. By having study and exploration be a part of your life, it will then, naturally, be a part of your children's lives.

Chapter Four

Children and Choices

Many of the unschooling skeptics I've spoken to are convinced that all children, if left to their own devices, are always going to make wrong choices. Perhaps if left completely to their own devices they would make many bad choices, but then again, I've never met a child left completely on their own. I believe we are given the responsibility by God to help our children make good and Holy decisions concerning their lives.

How do you know that your children will always make good choices regarding their lives and education? The truth is, you don't, and, trust me, they won't always make good decisions. But with forethought, guidance and prayer you will be able to partner with the Lord to help your children learn about the process of decision making and the consequences of those choices.

I once heard a wonderful sermon from an associate pastor regarding this subject. His basic premise was that a house with God at it's center, was a house that had a basis for its decisions and choices. I think that's a worthy goal, teaching our children to make choices pleasing to God. It's a goal that should be a priority for all Christians, not just children.

By Example

Throughout this book, I've emphasized my belief that the most important message we can give our children is an unspoken one. They watch us so carefully. My son is very adept at noticing incongruent behavior and isn't shy to ask me about it. While making important decisions, my husband

and I allow the children to see the process. By doing so we are showing them how it's done.

For example, when my husband and I noticed our morning family time becoming a bit chaotic, we sat down and reprioritized our days. We included our children in this process and decided that we had to make praying together and eating breakfast together one of our top priorities. As we talked, I realized that I was going to have to sacrifice checking my email first thing in the morning. When I agreed, the message I was sending about my priorities was clear. Family is important. When my husband chooses to go to worship practice instead of fishing, he is showing our children what he holds dear. By our choices, we show our children where our heart is.

Keeping this in mind gives us a powerful tool that will help our children learn to make good decisions. What will your children pick up if you choose to read rather then watch a favorite television show? Or if your husband occasionally takes the afternoon off to join them on a special field trip? Or if you go to church on Sundays instead of sleeping in? The number one tool we have for influencing our children's behavior is our own example.

By The Book

One of the most powerful ways God communicates his desires with us is by his Word. WWJD (What Would Jesus Do?) has been over-used and over-marketed, but it's still a powerful question if compared with what He *did* do in His ministry. When faced with tough choices, I have learned this is one of the top ways to find an answer. I want my children to look to the Word of God for guidance. To do so, they have to know the word of God, and that needs to be a constant in our lives. Philippians 4:8 is a wonderful verse for all of us to decide what we should allow in our lives.

Finally, Brethren, whatever things are true, whatever things are noble, whatever things just, whatever things are pure, whatever things are lovely, whatever things are of good report, if there is anything of virtue and if there is anything praiseworthy, meditate on these things. Philippians 4:8

This verse is probably the one most often used in our house when it comes to choosing what we should watch or listen to. The Bible is full of wisdom regarding what sort of behavior is pleasing to the Lord and what isn't. Teaching our children to use that wisdom is more than half the battle.

By Prayer

Praying over our days is a habit I'm trying hard to cultivate. I would love to teach my children how important it is to consult with the Lord over what to prioritize in their lives. I've found that praying, as I look over my planner, brings things into focus and is an effective way to make good decisions regarding how to use my time.

When faced with tough choices, prayer is often the only way to find an answer. I have prayed with my children when we were uncertain of what to do next or when something was amiss. Prayer is more than a rote tradition at mealtimes, it is a living experience.

Teaching children to pray is a skill they can take with them when they leave home and will hold them in good stead throughout their lives.

By Consequences

I've found allowing the natural consequences of a poor choice to be an effective manner in teaching my children about decisions. I've also discovered that I'm not real good at this one. My first instinct is to protect them from consequence. But real life consequences, provided they are not harmful physically, spiritually or mentally, are one of the best exercises in teaching God has ever utilized in my life.

The problem with consequences is that at times children are often not mature enough to understand the long term consequences of certain behaviors. They might not be able to see the results of exorbitant amounts of TV viewing, while we, as concerned parents, know the affects this activity can have physically and spiritually.

Natural consequences, within reason, can allow children the experience of their choices while still under the protection of their parents.

I feel it is imperative for children to realize the importance of developing good decision making skills, especially if you're allowing them both the freedom and responsibility of making a large portion of their educational choices. And just perhaps, the experiences gained while making those choices will turn out to be one of the most important factors in teaching children to make wise life decisions.

Chapter Five

The Worth of a Day

So many people have asked me, "So what does your family do all day?" that I have decided to include a chapter about a "typical" day at my house. I chose a day that was rather normal, some days we do more, some less.

I had been under the weather for a few days, so I didn't get up early to write as I usually do. I awoke at eight and my ten-year-old son had been up for an hour or so. He's my early riser, often getting up at 4:30 AM to shatter my early morning quiet.

He had already dressed, made his breakfast and fed and watered the rabbits. I grabbed my coffee and headed for the chair. My devotional time had been steadily disintegrating along with my health and today was no different. I grabbed my Bible and sat in the chair with my coffee, but that's as far as I got before my nine-year-old daughter dragged herself out of bed and headed for my lap. It seemed like a good morning to watch a movie.

I had checked out *The Long Walk Home*, from the library the night before. I hadn't seen it, but had been looking for movies that were culturally expanding, so to speak. Over the protests of my children, I put it in the VCR and turned it on. For the next two hours we were riveted to the television as this compelling story of the Birmingham bus boycott unfolded. At it's stunning conclusion, my children were full of questions. A lively discussion ensued until I finally put a stop to it realizing it was almost 11:00 AM and my daughter and I weren't even dressed yet. (I told you I was sick!)

We hurriedly got dressed and did the morning chores. After eating a quick breakfast I dragged myself out the door, along with the children, to get the materials needed for the clown costumes they were to wear for the Oregon Home Educators Network's talent show. Though they were to perform in a week, I'd been waiting till I felt better to get their costumes done. It didn't look like that was going to happen anytime soon and it needed to be done, whether I felt like it or not. We rushed around the fabric store, they helped choose what they needed and counted up the cost. The mall was next and we finished there in record time.

The mail had come while we were gone and, to my delight, both children had received something. Ethan had been looking for an opportunity to volunteer with the Oregon Fish and Wildlife department. The biologist I spoke to was very supportive and had added some study materials to the packet he sent. My son disappeared into his room to read for a couple of hours. My daughter got a magazine for girls and she sat down to read as much as she could. I decided to try to get some writing done.

After staring at a blank screen for a while, I got up and figured that I could be more productive cleaning. We had to practice their clown routine and when they both showed up looking for something new, I sent them off to get their clown hats. This was something I could do sitting in the recliner. We ran through the skits twice before dad showed up and took them off for a jog to the gym. I was then able to get some real work done.

I wasn't feeling well, so my husband fixed dinner while I laid on the couch. We put the movie in for Dad and watched it while eating. My son became tired before it finished and got up and went to bed. After Dad retired, I cleaned up the kitchen while Megan worked out some new moves to a song she had been making a dance for.

I sat down to complete an article that needed to be finished and Megan got out her money and started counting. I watched with fascination as she kept putting the change into different piles then rearranging them again. After I finished the article, we were both more than ready for bed.

Elissa's Day

Our days here vary from day to day, depending on what God has planned for us. I have three boys, two are seven-year-olds and one is six. I am currently pregnant, so life is always interesting. Two of the children are step-children and go to public school, but the other seven year old has been homeschooled since birth. We do have some things that are daily...like making beds, eating, getting stepsons off to school, retrieving them from school, bath time and prayers.

Other than that, we occupy ourselves with life. Our lives currently include a grandma going through chemotherapy, a pregnant mommy and house hunting. These three things offer us an almost nonstop opportunity for dialogue.

With grandma in and out of the hospital, we've had the chance to go to the military hospital to visit pretty often. We saw an air show there once, so we always get to talking about airplanes and military life in general. The chemotherapy has ravaged grandma's body, creating heart attacks and more, so we've had a lot of health discussions and anatomy talks.

My being pregnant has opened up the floodgates on child development. The children always want to know how big the baby is, what it is doing and when we will see it move. We utilize a great website that shows the stages of development in utero, and frequently we talk about the process of giving birth.

The other big thing in our lives right now is house hunting. We compare house/room/yard size, the pros and cons of one-story vs. two-story living, the idea of pool safety, the responsibilities of having one's own rooms and much more.

In between these busy life happenings, we have many cool learning opportunities. Reading is way at the top of our list. Somehow, without me "teaching" it, Brian is now reading. We've always had books around, read aloud, labeled things and sounded words out, well...it turned into reading. Everywhere we go, like Mother like son, there is a book waiting in the background. If not a book, a *Highlights* magazine or *Zoo Mag*!

I think daily learning tools can often be found in the home. The computer, CD ROMs, Legos, Monopoly, Trivial Pursuit, Bingo, field identification guides, crayons, coloring books, books, dictionaries, telephone books, newspaper, the Bible, a globe, atlases, rulers, calculators, clocks, measuring tapes, money, videotapes, rocks, microscope, pets, magnets, houseplants, thermometers, batteries, magnifying glass...the list is endless. The point is, we learn through life, and use life things.

Now, here's the key to our days—dialogue. We talk about everything and anything. I can say much of what my son has learned has come from pure talking. Discussions happen all the time...example 1) brushing teeth, asks about how mirrors work; 2) watching Scooby Doo, hears an unknown word, runs to me and asks me to explain it; 3)Finds a leaf, wants to know what tree it's from.

All these things lead to others...tree identification was a big thing here for a long time. We would find leaves, nuts and flowers, and determine what trees they came from. While looking through the field guide, we realized these trees don't live in the western hemisphere (geography), or they sure house a lot of different animals (life science), or count how many rings in this slice of tree (math)...what was happening when this tree was planted (history)...

I just can't stress how important talking is to my son's education. Use time in the car and quiet time before bed to drive in key points and reinforce beliefs.

What Will *Your* Day Include?

There are so many experiences to be had by staying aware. Each day holds the promise of new things to be learned. While we move in and out of our loose schedule we keep ourselves open for the serendipitous the Lord might have in store for us. How your days look depends on your family and circumstances. I pray they will be full of the joy of learning.

Chapter Six

A Round-Up of Ideas

There are many parents out there overflowing with creativity. Those who take to the delights of unschooling like a duck to water, full of incredibly creative ideas to jump start their children's imaginations. Then there are those of us who stand there and say... duh. Most of us are the products of a system that has all but dried up our innovation. I am including this chapter for those parents who are creatively challenged. Once you get the hang of unschooling, the sky's the limit for both your potential and your child's.

Language Arts

Louisa May Alcott. Even to this day, just hearing that name sends me back to my childhood. I remember perching myself on an immense boulder out in the middle of my Grandmother's pasture. It was by far the most wonderful place to read and I spent many hours there, book in hand, with an apple tucked away for snacking. It was there I first met Lousia May Alcott, not through the books she wrote, but through a small biography of her life. I read it over and over, enchanted more by her life story than by her works. It was on that boulder, I first determined to become a writer.

When I had children of my own, I began reading to them, practically in utero. My mission was not to raise geniuses, but to raise children who loved to read. When I began homeschooling, the habit of reading stood us well. Much of our learning is based on what we read. Now that my children are older I see the benefits.

My son possesses an extensive vocabulary. At ten he uses the words precisely, incidentally and exquisite, correctly and with ease. My children can understand cultural references with accuracy. "I know where that one's from," is a common phrase when they hear something we've formerly read in a book. Now that my son is reading well on his own, I can often find him, nose buried in a book, living out an adventure in a far away place. My daughter has transferred her love of reading into a love of writing and has several stories going at once.

The difference in attitude about education in my children versus those children who are not regularly read to, is incredible. Research shows that parental attitudes have a profound affect on your child's interest in learning to read. Children who learn from parents that reading is fun are more likely to sustain interest when the road to reading becomes difficult.

Learning to read is a much simpler job if the child already loves to be read to. Whether you belong to the phonics camp or the whole reading camp, a child who wants to learn to read, will read, no matter what method is used.

Other Ideas For Language Arts:

- Make labels for common household items together, decorate and place around the house.
- Read the Laura Ingalls Wilder books or books on other time periods and make a meal of some of the same foods.
- Act out a favorite story.

"One of the things that I have noticed with our almost hands off approach to language arts is that children who are read great literature speak well and articulately. Both of my children have incredible vocabularies without the tedious use of vocabulary lists. Besides, I never got to read this great stuff and I'm enjoying it right along with them!" Leanne Ely, North Carolina

"My favorite Language Arts idea is having my son dictate a story or book to me. After all of his words are down on paper, I read it back to him, word by word and he types it out on the word processor, working on his typing, spelling, capitalizing, punctuation etc." Michele Hastings, Canada

History

One of the best ways my family has found to learn about history is field trips. They just seem to go together, probably because of all those musty historical museums we were forced through when we were kids. If you haven't been to a museum lately, you're in for a big surprise. Most have come into the modern age and are far more interactive than they used to be. And even musty old museums are more interesting if you can linger where you like and leave when you want.

Though we love exploring old forts and museums, some of the best historical field trips have come from just exploring the country side. We've stopped at old towns, far off the beaten path, to discover ancient school houses and shops. On one trip across the Oregon high desert, we stopped at old homesteads. The lack of water and desolation of the landscape told the tale of families struggling to carve out a niche. Often we would find the root cellar and the garden plots just beyond the house. Sometimes we would talk of the family, imagining how many people lived there by how many rooms we counted in the house. We'd wonder what had happened to them, whether they lost the farm or simply moved somewhere more hospitable. Sometimes the children and I would see a prosperous ranch house, just beyond the old homestead, and wonder if it was an extension of the same family. Flights of fancy? Perhaps, but the enjoyable imaginings gave my children the opportunity to see real people behind the artifacts and history books.

Other Ideas For History

- Books lend themselves easily to the study of history. Family reading aloud times, historical biographies, Usborne books and the American Girl series are all interesting ways to read about history.
- Check your local historical society for upcoming events.
- There are many good computer games, videos, CDs and tapes on historical subjects. PBS, the Discovery Channel and other

television programs can be surefire ways to involve your children in history.

- Travel is a fun way to learn history. Call the Chamber of Commerce of your destination and ask for contact information of the local historical society. Learn about the history of your destination ahead of time to make the trip more enjoyable and educational.

"When I think back on what I learned about history from my own childhood, the most lasting memories are from research I wanted to do after reading historical novels. I wanted to know whether being a Mountie was REALLY like it said in Mrs. Mike, how accurately the gold rush was portrayed in Call of the Wild, and whether life in ancient Rome was what Ben Hur said it was. I don't remember much at all from any schoolbooks on history, but the novels formed lasting impressions in my mind that stick with me today." Kim Ohara, Washington

"For history, we made a timeline with continuous computer paper, (so it folds neatly back into a box), with each horizontal page representing a century. As my children read books about different time periods or people, they mark an interesting event or date from the book onto the timeline in its proper place. Sometimes they will draw a small picture or paste a small photo representing an event or person." Peggy Kremers, Arkansas

"Make history real, bring along a great historical biography or picture book relevant to the subject and read it on the spot! The words come alive when you're surrounded by the place and environment it took place at. We read 'The Fourth of July Story' sitting on a bench in the middle of Philadelphia just blocks away from Independence Hall. Another meaningful historical learning time was reading 'Make Way for Ducklings' sitting in front of the bronze ducklings in Boston's Public Garden." Kristy Kronz, Maryland

Math

I have to make a confession here. I am writing about a subject that I, personally, don't get. When it comes to math, most unschoolers seem to be confused and not sure how to approach it. Do we break down and use a curriculum for math? Ignore it and hope it goes away? Just how do you go about unschooling math anyway?

For me, the answer was very, very carefully! I was almost afraid to do anything at all, I didn't want to pass my phobia of this particular subject on to my children. We tried different programs, but none seemed to work. They went against my unschooling mentality, and my children were bored. Lots of people have had success with the Miquon math program. My children were ambivalent towards it. On one hand, they felt the cuisenaire rods were too babyish, and on the other, the book went too quickly for them. They barely had time to grasp one concept before jumping to another. Many unschoolers have liked Miquon, allowing the children to work at their own pace and interest level. I was back to square one.

So I ignored it. We blithely went on our historical field trips, did our nature studies, found new and intriguing ways to play with science, spent hours at the library and generally enjoyed our lives ... without math. I would only think of math when my husband gently prodded me, "Are they getting math anywhere?" he would ask late at night "Mmmhhhmmm," I would mumble and turn over and go to sleep.

When I saw a math workshop being offered at our state wide homeschool conference I jumped at the chance to attend. I knew the woman teaching was an avid unschooler who would give a good workshop. It turned out to be more than good, it was eye opening. It helped me to look at math with something besides fearful dread.

I learned that children must go through different stages before they can grasp various concepts. To insist that they learn facts before understanding the concepts is a recipe for math phobia. She also gave a lot of great ideas for setting up real world experiences. I was challenged to see the importance of math. After much thought, my husband and I came to the conclusion that we wanted our children to leave our home knowing survival or consumer math, how to balance a check book, calculate interest and comparison shop. If they needed higher math for a career goal, well, that was up to them. Inspired, I left the conference ready to tackle and tame the math dilemma.

First off, I went out and bought my children some calculators. I learned that not only does using a calculator require some basic understanding of math, but also sharpens those skills. They were delighted with their new calculators and we decided to try them out right away. One of the activities recommended at the conference was taking the children to buy their own lunches for a week. I handed them each ten dollars and told them "HEALTHY" and they were off. I think they learned more in that one trip than all the previous grocery shopping trips. It's an activity that we plan on repeating every month.

My children have always disliked manipulatives, at least for any purpose they might have been meant for. The counting bears I bought when they were younger have been used for everything under the sun, from cat toys to bombs used to destroy one another's Lincoln Log forts. The only thing they weren't used for was counting! Many children like pattern blocks, used to create designs and give an introduction to geometry. The abacus can be used for number placement and simple math problems. The secret in using manipulatives is not to get hung up on how they're supposed to be used. It once drove my crazy when the children wouldn't do what the book said to do. When I realized how much they were learning without the directions, I threw the book away.

I also got hold of a wonderful book called, *The I Hate Mathematics Book*. This book helped me think of math in a whole different way. It is written at a third grade reading level and is chock full of fun things to do with math. To my surprise, there were many fun ideas. My children seem to be enjoying themselves and I finally believe I'll be able to send them off into the world knowing a thing or two about consumer math.

Other Ideas For Math

- Let your children utilize some real life math such as balancing the checkbook, opening a savings account or holding a garage sale.
- Water play using measuring cups and cooking are fun ways to learn measurement.
- Learning about flight, making simple graphs and drawing maps all use and teach skills needed for higher math.
- Dividing up candy, pizza, pie etc. is a delicious way to learn fractions.

"My favorite Math idea is taking my kids into a store, (like Pokey's Tackle Shop where there are trays and trays of fishing paraphernalia) and having them add up their selections in their heads, getting as close to the allotted amount of money as possible without going over." Michele Hastings, Canada

"My favorite math idea is having counters of all types available. Creative, economical things like macaroni, buttons or paperclips." Leanne Ely, North Carolina

"My favorite idea for math is: Shortcuts! All shapes, all sizes. A junior high teacher told me once that all true mathematicians are lazy: They like to find easier ways to do things. I teach my kids to use (and find their own) shortcuts, whenever I can." Kim Ohara, Washington

"I've never understood the concept of buying "fake" money when the real thing is so much more meaningful for our children. Teach by really doing it! Before you venture into a real store set up a pretend store in your home and let the children buy and spend accordingly. They'll learn the names and amounts of the coins through their own experiences and will soon be ready for the responsibility of buying goods on their own accord (with a little supervision of course)." Kristy Kronz, Maryland

Science

Geeks and Goggles, Beakers and Boredom ... sounds like a witch's brew. For me it was a recipe for a nightmare. I detested it when I was in school. The experiments had all been done before and the emphasis was on filling out your lab book and not discovery. I was determined it would be different for my children. The problem was, I had no idea how to make it different. Was there a way to teach science without beakers and boredom? Or, more specifically, without teaching it at all?

I wasn't satisfied with the text books I had perused on the subject. They looked too much like my old science or biology books. I wanted something different. Something I would be as interested in as the children. Floundering, I made the decision to put it off and just do nature study for a while. I thought with any luck neither of my kids would be interested in hard core science.

A word of advice: if you want to raise children who have no interest in science, don't do nature studies! We'd ramble for hours with binoculars and sketch books, examining plants, mushrooms and berries. Sometimes we'd take a picnic lunch to see what specimens of insects could be attracted by the scent of our peanut butter sandwiches. My son, being fascinated by insects, wanted to create a bug collection, like his father had when he was a boy. His little sister had other ideas, however. She freed everything he caught before he had a chance to euthanize them, giving us a lesson in humane education.

My children moved delightedly from one branch of science to another without realizing it. A nearby marsh became a passion for several months with the children filling containers with murky water to see what water bugs they could find. We caught and watched the miracle of tadpoles turning to frogs and dug up cat tails to see what their roots looked like. I found a wonderful book, *The Handbook of Nature Study*, by Anna Botsford Comstock. It is filled with gentle lessons in studying the natural world and though we didn't follow the lessons, the tips and information were invaluable.

Television seemed to conspire against me as well, airing shows that were designed to hook children on science. 'Bill Nye the Science Guy' and 'The Magic School Bus' further inspired them to conduct a myriad of experiments. The Kratts Brothers turned my son into a walking animal encyclopedia who could spout off the names, habits and classifications of obscure animals. Actually, television has taught my kids more science then I ever could. They graduated from 'Magic School Bus' to 'Nova' in a blink of an eye and I knew I was going to have to become more and more creative in my efforts to keep my scientifically hungry children satisfied.

The library was my science savior. Having no interest in the subject myself, I endeavored to discover science books my children could use on their own. *The Back Yard Science* books were ideal. All I had to do was make sure they had lots of materials on hand and that they cleaned up the mess. At the time my son was reading and could follow the directions on his own and spell out words for his sister. I was spared... for the moment. Another excellent book my children love is *Magic Science*, by Jim Wiese. Combining children's love of magic with science was a brilliant idea. Even I was interested in this one! We created a disappearing penny, a broken pencil that wasn't broken and scared pepper. After each trick there's a scientific explanation of what you've just done.

Science can pop up in the most unlikely places. My husband's passion for fishing was passed on to my children and before we knew it my son was well versed on the life cycles of salmon and steelhead. Hoping to foster this interest, we took a field trip up to a dam on the Columbia river. After approximately an hour of wandering through the hatchery, my son fell in love and became determined to spend the rest of his life saving our native salmon runs. He embarked on a writing campaign to fishing guides, inquiring about their opinions on common hatchery practices. Counting the years until he was old enough to volunteer at nearby hatcheries, he pressed me into finding out what type of degree he would need to work in the field and how long it would take him to obtain it.

My daughter, artistic by nature, spends a great deal of her time sketching animals in their natural habitats. She has recently become interested in photography, not just in taking pictures but the whole science of it. I am waiting for the day when she will announce that she needs a dark room!

Other Ideas For Science

- Caring for a garden is a great hands on way to learn about science.
- Get a telescope to look at the sky or get a microscope and look at anything.
- Train those powers of observation by bird watching, weather watching, cloud watching or even bug watching.

"My favorite science idea is researching, via books and the Internet, a pet...and then going out and making all the necessary purchases and taking care of that pet." Michele Hastings, Canada

"We have tried the boring science text books, but it just doesn't work in my house. I have a couple of Usborne books that I refer to for science experiments, but what I use most often is Robert Krampf's Experiment of the Week. These experiments are available in book form as well as email form. They are super, inexpensive and thought provoking!" Patricia Newton, New Jersey

"Make science an everyday experience. The great outdoors is one big learning arena. Just take a walk, talk about what you see and notice changes. Then go home and read about it. We found a bird's nest made of hair just recently. This led to a discussion of animals native to our area (who's hair it might be), then to farming, then to types of bird's nests, and finally to a book about birds and their nesting preferences. We were armed with this knowledge when on the next day we found a nest made of mud and could easily identify the barn swallow who made it." Kristy Kronz, Maryland

Chapter Seven

Teaching versus Facilitating

"I've always thought of teaching as imparting something I already know; facilitating, on the other hand, is helping to learn something along with my child. I think "teach" is also used negatively, as in "forced teaching," while "facilitate" is less loaded with our own public school baggage. My son, age five or so at the time, told me in no uncertain terms: 'Don't ever teach me anything again! You make it more confusing!' An unschooler was born." Nancy Wooten, California

One of the things that many people don't understand about unschooling is the concept of teaching versus facilitating. The difference is subtle, often blending. Teaching is something parents have been doing for their children since birth. Facilitating is also something we have been doing since birth. The trick is trying to figure out which situations call for which method.

When we slowly and patiently showed our children to tie their shoes... we were teaching. When we helped our children speak, by speaking clearly to them, we were facilitating. Facilitating is a combination of teaching and encouragement. You encourage children to discover things on their own, provide them the tools to do it, and the means to make their learning possible.

What is a Facilitator?

"As a facilitator, I would bring my children in contact with something and help them relate to it... converse with them... ask questions... point out interesting things... as a teacher, I would sit them down and lecture them... fill their heads

with facts and information rather than allowing them to access and relate to the materials themselves." Debi Taylor-Hough, Washington

When you facilitate your child's interest in science, for example, you give them ideas on how to learn more about science. You can suggest a trip to the library or offer to find them a community class on the subject. You leave the choice up to them and make it possible when they do choose. I suggested to my son that we ask our veterinarian if he could observe some surgeries. After thinking about it for several days my son agreed that was something he would like to do. I made the phone calls, set up the time and drove him to the appointment. If he were older I would have let him do those things, but at 10 he wanted me to do the actual asking and scheduling. That is facilitating a child's interest.

Being Your Child's Facilitator

Facilitating means being a good resource for your child. Finding mentors that will nurture your child's interest without being too schoolish is tricky, but it can be done. The veterinarian mentioned above, allowed my son to observe, answered questions and permitted learning to happen. As more and more people become familiar with homeschooling, opportunities like this will be more common.

> *"My belief (and I've only come to this conclusion after having children and unschooling them from birth), is that teaching should be the act of enabling/facilitating a love of learning. Nothing more, nothing less. If teaching involves forcing information into a child's brain—then it is counterproductive. Rather, by providing an environment and objects all around (God does a wonderful job of this!) and having a spirit and attitude of joy and excitement about all that you are learning yourself, your child's learning will be a natural result.* Kristy Kronz, Maryland

Please don't misunderstand me, I am not saying that teaching is wrong or unhealthy. Teaching our children is, I believe, a mandate from God. But for me, one of the most important parts of unschooling or raising children is teaching my children to teach themselves what they need to know.

> *"I feel that teaching has an expected time and outcome, whereas facilitating leaves the learning door wide open so that individual thinking and timing is permitted. This way the student is allowed to see the subject at a different angles than we do but still understand." Alice Steen, Georgia*

Facilitating is allowing your children the freedom to access learning materials and the time to explore those materials without an agenda. Teaching often gets in the way of actual learning. If a child is not ready for the particular piece of information the parent is trying to impart, then the child will not retain that information. It won't matter how wonderful the teaching materials or persistent the parent. If, instead, the parent allows the child to play with the materials, freely and without restrictions, the child's own exploration often leads to a readiness for the very information the parent wishes the child to learn. It is often a matter of timing and personal readiness.

> *"When you're teaching, you are initiating the learning experience. When you're facilitating, the student is the one initiating the learning experience...you're just providing requested information. You're showing them what they want to know...instead of showing them what you want them to know. In facilitating, they see the significance of what they're learning and their desire to know the information makes them a much more receptive vessel." Michele Hastings, Canada*

There are as many ways to facilitate a child's learning as there are to teach a child. Each child is an individual in their thoughts and learning patterns. Teaching academics is much different than teaching how to make brownies or teaching the love of learning. Of course, the best way to teach your children to love learning is to facilitate it.

True learning takes place when a love of learning is established and it is established by facilitating and not teaching. Some people feel facts need to be taught, but they are much easier caught by a child who loves to learn.

> *"Children have such an innate power and desire to learn. They are human sponges, and can often soak up more than we have to offer! Why not take advantage of this from birth by having a lifestyle of learning in your every moment together? This facilitating of learning and growing and becoming together is what God intended when He created family." Kristy Kronz, Maryland*

Chapter Eight

Learning to Lean on Spirit

Sometimes I think about how Jesus taught the disciples. If you think about it, they were in a sense, unschoolers. They followed Him, ate with Him, worked with Him and listened to Him. It is important to realize that He didn't teach them to read and write, He taught them about faith. He taught them about His Father.

In attempting to follow Christ, I've emulated His example in teaching the Christian faith to my children. The things of the Spirit are so intertwined in our lives that just in the course of the day's activities, I find many chances to teach my children about Christ. Why should I get my children a curriculum packet to teach my faith when Christ did not have one for His disciples? How can you teach a living, breathing faith if you are teaching out of a book that is not the Bible? How the Word addresses our day is what makes it relevant to our children. How can we please God today with our actions? That is what they need to know.

To bestow upon my children the gift of my faith is why the Lord has given them to me. It is my most important mission, not something to take lightly. I look to the Bible to find the clearest illustration of this process, the years that Christ took a crew of mostly uneducated men and turned them into men of faith. Men our God used for His perfect purpose. I know I cannot be the most perfect of teachers... but I will try to imitate Him. That is why I am here.

Unschooling Christianity?

So, exactly how does one go about being a Christian and an unschooler with the job of passing your faith on to your children? The children's programs offered by churches didn't seem to work for us. I was of the mind if my children wanted such and such a patch or star they would learn what was necessary. My son did. My daughter didn't. Soon my daughter was complaining that the teachers kept asking her why we didn't work harder in her book. Then my son began feeling bad because he wasn't memorizing three to four verses a week like his friends were. The competitiveness of the world doesn't stop at the sanctuary doors and is often passed down to children from the parent. My husband and I have determined that we would rather have our children truly *live* one Bible verse then be able to recite hundreds.

We find the Bible has far more impact on our children when we use it to shed light on the complexities of life. I find that my children retain the truths of the Bible better if they have come to it full of questions and hungry for answers.

My son, especially, loves the stories and rich traditions he finds in the Bible. The stories of Samson, Noah and Abraham ellicit wonderful discussions and, inevitably, further study. My daughter prefers the works of Christ.

"Mama, did the five thousand like the dry fish and flat bread?" she once asked.

"I don't know, honey, I suspect, since that was all they had, they liked it well enough."

"Why was that all they had?"

"They were, for the most part, very poor and they had been there for several days."

"Why were they poor?"

From diapers to social worker in the space of a year. Who says unschooling doesn't work? Now that my children are older, we often take turns reading the Bible and discussing what we read. Then we take part of what we've read and try to apply it to our lives.

Another way we unschool our faith is by pointing out to one another where God's finger is in our individual lives. Where do we see him working? We take the power of prayer seriously and pray together often. Not formula prayer, but rather spontaneous prayer, when we feel the need to touch base with our Creator. Though we generally avoid rote prayer, there are times when praying the Psalms hits a spiritual nerve. The words are lovely, rich and full of life.

It was a heart hunger that led me to Christ and a relationship with God and I believe this identical heart hunger will pull our children in the same direction. My husband was the worship leader of a youth group for several years and we saw it time and time again. Teens who were apathetic about God coming to some private turning point in lives, then being lit up with the Spirit. At this time they begin to actively seek out spiritual things in a quest for answers. I believe at some time our children will come to a crossroads... a juncture in which they will have to make their parents' faith their own or not. The Lord gave all people free will to choose to follow Him or not. Our children will have to make that choice on their own, a choice made deep inside their own soul. We can lead and guide, love and pray, but when it comes to salvation we can't do it for them.

So what does knowing God and unschooling Christianity have to do with how your children are educated? Everything. In being Christian unschoolers, we have made a choice on what is important to us: God's continuing work in our children. Trusting that He will let us know how to partner with Him in raising our children. Leaning on Him. In being Christians, we know that character development is just as important as our children's education. All of the education and money in the world will not benefit the person who loses his soul.

I began this chapter by looking at the way Christ taught the disciples. I will end it with a verse from the Old Testament.

For the Lord gives wisdom;
From His mouth come knowledge
and understanding. Proverbs 2:6 NKJV

In the words of the preacher, *"Vanity, vanities, all is vanity."* Because God is the most important thing in this life, when it comes right down to it, all else is just vanity. Whatever else your education is, it needs to begin and end with God.

Chapter Nine

Records and Record Keeping

Probably the most confusing part of unschooling is the keeping of records. We have had so many questions regarding this topic that we've decided to devote a chapter to the subject.

For compliancy, one should start with local laws and work within these guidelines. For many unschoolers, portfolios seem to be the favored way of keeping records. These are notebooks with work samples, records of subjects studied and special activities noted. Keeping a daily journal, as described in Chapter Three, also works. However, I know many people who prefer to keep a weekly journal rather than a daily one. Parent written evaluations are another way to keep records. They are used either by themselves or in conjunction with a portfolio depending on state requirements. The following is an actual evaluation written by a parent for the sole purpose of complying to state regulations. The name has been changed for the privacy of the child.

Grade 6 1999-2000 School Year

Language Arts

David enjoys reading. He was interested in the Animorphs series of books and read several of them in the fall. As a challenge, he read *The Hobbit* by JRR Tolkien. His tastes run to the fantasy and science fiction genre. Grammar is done orally, with corrections made by either myself, his dad or his grandparents. During our many trips either in the car or on a jet, we use Mad Libs for reinforcing parts of speech. We usually challenge him to find interesting and unusual words for the Mad Libs. David has also used the *Comprehensive Curriculum of Basic Skills* - Grade 6 by American Education Publishing for homographs, reading comprehension, spelling, thinking skills, punctuation and grammar. Another source for reading comprehension was a booklet called *High-Interest Reading* by Walter Hazen. David read the non-fiction stories in this book which brought about discussion and further study.

Math

David used the Comprehensive Curriculum of Basic Skills to sharpen his math skills. He also used consumer math and math challenges that he set up himself. David is very quick with math and has an intuitive sense of numbers. He likes to challenge himself with math questions and we like to challenge him as well. Most math is done orally as he can do most in his head. He has rolled coins and added up the result for one of our car trips. David also likes to figure out grocery totals and change. Many times fractions have been learned through cooking with either doubling or halving recipes. David is fascinated with banking and how banks work. We have spent many days discussing the banking system and how money is used. Our family tiled about 500 square feet of our house, and David was shown how we came to the amount of square feet using geometry. David has a high interest in magic tricks and has been learning some of the "tricks" in the book *Mathemagic* by Raymond Blum.

Science

David has a high interest in science. We used many science experiment kits including *Stinky, Smelly, Hold-Your-Nose Science* by Scholastic, and *Icky, Sticky, Foamy, Slimy, Ooey, Gooey Chemistry* also from Scholastic. We also used *Physical Science* by Frank White trying several experiments including dancing macaroni, bouncing eggs and dissolving a nail. Many of our trips have included science, like a trip to the Florida Aquarium in Tampa, the National Aquarium in Baltimore, a guided nature walk on the shores of the bay on Cape Cod by the Cape Cod Museum of Natural History, a self-guided tour of the Massachusetts Audubon Society Wellfleet Bay Wildlife Sanctuary, a day-long visit to Drumhaller and the Royal Tyrrell Museum in Alberta, Canada, a world-class dinosaur museum and our passes to Sea World. While in Calgary, Alberta we drove to Banff where we saw coyote and elk on the side of the road. We also drove to Lake Louise where we were able to see three glaciers on the mountain. The drive to Drumhaller took us to several canyons on the seemingly flat farmland. We were also able to see several more coyotes on the drive to Edmonton and we saw magpies for the first time. David volunteers at the Orlando Science Center.

History

David has continued his interest in Ancient Egypt and we have visited the Royal Ontario Museum in Toronto, with an emphasis on the Egyptian collection. This collection included actual mummies. We also added to the Egyptian study with a tour of the Egyptian collection at the Metropolitan Museum of Art in New York City. This collection included a restored Temple of Dendur, which had graffiti from the 19th century explorers and adventurers who had discovered it. Another interest of study was ancient man and we used the book, *Step Into…The Stone Age* by Charlotte Hurdman. This book had many hands-on activities including making a hunting spear and clay pots. We did a brief study of ancient Greece which will continue on for the next school year. Another area of study was about the Vikings where we read the book *Step Into… The Viking World* by Philip Steele. This was also enriched by the TV program on NOVA called The Vikings. We had visited one area the Vikings had landed, Newfoundland, and the kids were very interested in this aspect. Our history education was enriched with visits to the Royal Tyrrell Museum in Alberta, Canada; the Metropolitan Museum of Art in New York City; and Royal Ontario Museum in Toronto, Ontario, Canada. A more modern history was discovered when we saw the play "The Diary of Anne Frank". This led to many discussions of Hitler and WWII. The evening after viewing the play my parents had a very good friend over who was Jewish and from Germany and had lost his whole family to the concentration camps. This led to some interesting and very sad discussion.

Geography

Our study of geography stems from our travel. We use the *Rand McNally Road Atlas of the US and Canada*, and the *Rand McNally Premier World Atlas.* Other sources of geography comes from *National Geographic* magazine and maps. We usually buy a map of every area we plan on visiting and consult that map often. Both of the kids are good map readers and have been our navigators on many trips. We have added to our history study with a study of the geography of the area. Our trips have included a driving trip to New Jersey, then on to New Hampshire and the Lake Winnipesaukee area and on again to Cape Cod, Massachusetts. Our next trip was a flight to Toronto, Ontario and several visits to the city and suburbs. In December we flew to Calgary, Alberta and drove to Banff, Lake Louise Drumhaller, and Edmonton to the world's largest enclosed mall. In May we visited New Jersey and New York with a visit to New York City using maps of the city and the bus system. The kids also helped us find our way in upstate New York during a severe thunderstorm.

Computer Science

David is very interested in computers. We have a peer to peer network in our house and David has been involved in the building/rebuilding of our home computers. He installs/uninstalls software, uses Windows 98, shares files through the peer-to-peer network, and troubleshoots his own computer. He is currently in the middle of a Visual Basic programming class being taught at home through the South-Western company.

Physical Education

David swims in our pool, roller blades, boogie boards at the beach and has done some light hiking both in Florida and in the Banff snow. While in Calgary he took a 90-minute snowboarding lesson and went snowboarding again the next day.

Miscellaneous Activities/Classes - (1) David was involved in training our puppy. We all took the puppy training class through Friends Fur

Life. (2) David attended the beginning Sign Language class through Homeschool Network and used the book, *Signing Illustrated, the Complete Learning Guide* by Mickey Flodin. David and his sister use sign often with each other, mostly finger spelling. (3) David has also begun volunteering for the Orlando Science Center on Wednesdays from 9am to 4pm. (4) We have visited the Merritt Island National Wildlife Refuge, Blue Springs State Park to see manatees, Wekiwa Springs State Park and Hontoon Island State Park.

As you can see by the previous evaluation, almost any and all activities your children participate in can be used in creating very professional evaluations. The trick is to use "educationalese" whenever possible. For instance, if you and your children take a nature walk in the park you are doing science and PE. Family reading can become English, history, vocabulary development and developing listening skills. Remember to keep your records as professional and polished as possible.

Record Keeping Resources

The Harris Homeschool Planner includes teacher and student planners and record keeping notebooks. For more information write or call: Harris Homeschool Resources, P.O. Box 24, Richmond, ME 04357 Phone (207) 737-0983

And What About College by Cafi Cohen, Prima Publishing 1999. Walks you right through what to save, how to phrase things and what categories to put information under. She shows how to save all of our learning experiences!

The Home School Source Book by Donn Reed, Offers many forms and more. For more information write to Brook Farm Books, P.O. BOX 246, Bridgewater, ME 04735.

The Essays

We now come to the heart and soul of our book. We could talk ourselves breathless and many would still have doubts about the validity of unschooling. These essays are written by Christians from across the United States and Canada, who have chosen unschooling for their families. In the following pages you will get to know these families, their successes, their doubts, their different lifestyles and reasons for unschooling.

First, let me explain part of how we chose the essays for our book. Early on, in our gathering of contributions, we had one woman tell us that while she would very much like to contribute, she wasn't sure that she should. When asked the reason for her hesitance, she stated that she was a Catholic and had been told by some Christians that she wasn't a true Christian. We quickly told her that if she believed in the Lord Jesus Christ, and had given her life to him, she was a Christian. This incident brought to our attention a problem that might come up. Did we have the right or the resources to check out every contributor's claim that they were Christian? Or to pass judgment on what kind of Christianity they practiced?

After much prayer and thought we decided that we did not have the right nor were we, in any form, going to have our contributors sign a statement of faith. Both of us detest the type of separation that has come about within the church due to quibbling over doctrine or small bits of scripture. We realized that there might come, at some point, a person or group of people who will disagree with this. Be that as it may, this is our stand.

Another point of contention is the purity of unschooling that these families may or may not represent. Most unschoolers have, at one point or another, used a workbook or part of a curriculum. Some occasionally still do. Sometimes this is because of the insecurities or doubts that occasionally beset us all, (even many of those who use a curriculum all the time have doubts about their choice to homeschool) and sometimes it is because there is something very important to us, that we as parents, wanted our children to know. Some families may have children who love to work out of workbooks, find certain textbooks fascinating, or perhaps have a life goal that will take more formal schooling. We have rejected a few essays because we could not see any evidence of unschooling. But for the most part, we have chosen to be a bit lenient on this point. The main criteria for us was to include essays where the children seemed to have a great deal of freedom and input in their educational choices.

The people who have written for us, have generously given their time and their stories so that other parents can see that unschooling does work as a choice and faith filled Christians are practicing it. Please read these essays with the same faith and generosity with which they were written and may you be blessed by them.

Chapter Ten

Why We Unschool

People turn to unschooling for various reasons. Some fall into it while others choose it as a means of combating "school at home" burnout. Still others have done extensive research and feel unschooling is the best way for their children to be educated. As Christians, most, if not all, of our essay contributors unschool because they feel this is the path God is leading them down. For my family, we came to unschooling after trying the "school at home" method and realizing that we were all miserable with it. For Elissa's family, unschooling came as naturally as breathing, something they always practiced.

What about education is important to you? What is important for your children to learn? Where is God leading your children? The following essays show how diverse Christian families are in how they feel about unschooling.

What I Want for My Children

by Deborah Taylor-Hough

I remembered all too well the long hours spent idly during my own childhood sitting in school reading dry-as-dust textbooks, studying only to pass the test, learning to play the "game" of pleasing the teacher, and always feeling that there was so much more out there in life to learn about, ponder and experience.

I want so much more for my own children.

As Charlotte Mason taught in the last century, children are born persons. They are not possessions, nor a cog in the machine, nor simply a warm body to feed and clothe. They are individuals with a spark of life all their own—their own dreams, desires, spiritual hunger and gifts. Children have capable minds to be respected, not devalued with "twaddle" or dumbed down literature.

I remember as a child being frustrated by 'Sesame Street' when it first came on the air back in the sixties. I was only about seven or eight at the time, but I can remember sitting in front of the television with my two younger next-door neighbors and feeling horrified by the twaddle being paraded in front of my eyes. Why should I watch something ridiculous like that when I could curl up with Beatrix Potter or any number of favorite authors and have my imagination encouraged and my heart enlarged?

And oftentimes I thought, "Why watch television at all when there was so much important playing to be done?" I believe that play is an important—no, essential—part of childhood. In the book, *For the Children's Sake*, Susan Schaeffer MaCauley writes, "One of the saddest things I know is to watch students at L'Abri look at a group of children, involved for hours in satisfying play, and comment, 'I've never seen children playing like that.' No? Then weep. Even childhood is robbed of the richness of humanity."

I remember the long afternoon hours of play on our street where I grew up. Mud pies were the feast of the day, impromptu races of various sorts kept us active and healthy, relaxed ball games that included everyone (even the youngest or least coordinated of the children), building forts, driving our "motorcycles" (i.e.: tricycles), and even acting out our own made-up scenes from 'Gilligan's Island' with all the neighborhood children playing their favorite characters. I know I could rightly argue that watching 'Gilligan's Island' in the first place was a rather non-educational event, but the natural play that occurred as we acted out our roles was important.

I always wanted to play the Professor. He was one of my childhood heroes. Any man who could make a radio out of coconuts and spend his day surrounded by test tubes and beakers, never losing his logical take on life, was someone after my own heart (I was a rather odd kid!).

Odd, maybe. But I was me—totally individual in my thinking and make up. And I think that takes us back to the idea of children being born persons. Fortunately, no one came and interrupted our well-developed game and said that I couldn't play the Professor since I was a girl. I was allowed to give free reign to my imagination and fully explore, through the simple joys of play, what I thought it would mean to be a scientist as an adult. (By the way, as an adult I did end up working in a medical laboratory—surrounded by test tubes and beakers!). Maybe playing 'Gilligan's Island' seems a bit silly, but we played with all our hearts and it was a game totally of our own devising, no adults telling us what to do or how to do it.

Now-a-days, the myriad of organized sports and outside activities that children participate in from preschool on up (I know elementary age children carrying Day Planners to keep track of all their activities) bombard kids. It seems to be almost the antithesis of that healthy, hearty, spontaneous and child directed play that goes into shaping the character, dreams and thoughts of an individual, growing person.

Another important memory from my own childhood is my grandmother baby-sitting me often when I was quite young. Each night she'd read one of the Beatrix Potter books to me. Those moments curled up, warm under the covers with Grandma sitting on a chair beside the guest bed reading delightful stories about Peter Rabbit, Tom Kitten and Benjamin Bunny are some of the warmest and fondest memories I hold dear from my childhood. Even now, reading those books to my own children evokes happiness in the deepest part of my being.

I think reading often and at length from good books, "living" books, chosen carefully for their literary value—interesting, educational and pleasurable to read, is one of the most valuable activities our family enjoys. I started reading aloud to my children when they were just days old. I knew they couldn't understand what I was reading yet, but I also knew that the love and care communicated to them by being held in my arms as

I read softly to them was a gift beyond measure. By the time my children were about three years old, they were all able to sit and listen to chapter books like *Charlotte's Web* or the original A.A.Milne classic, *Winnie-the-Pooh.*

I think I'll probably keep on reading aloud to my children for as long as they're living in my home. And then I hope to be able to read to my grandbabies someday, as well. I think all the reading aloud in our home has done wonders for our family. It has served as a treasured family activity, a foundation for a love of great literature in the children, a means for developing a stronger command of the language and an avenue for increasing listening skills.

By allowing our children to flourish at home, learning from the great minds of men and women who have gone before us, I believe their lives will be enriched, their hearts enlarged and their world touched by their dedicated lives. I want my children to feast their hearts, souls and minds on fine literature, awe-inspiring art, majestic music and great thoughts. I want them to learn how to think—not just learn to pass a test. I want them to be prepared spiritually, intellectually, morally and academically to pursue wholeheartedly whatever passion God laid on their hearts for the future, whether in the field of medicine, art, missions or homemaking. I believe a natural approach to education and life will accomplish many of these goals.

And that's what I want for my children.

Journeys

by Carol D Wickwire

We began our homeschool journey about a year and a half ago. We withdrew our four children from public school one at a time, each for different reasons. In hindsight, this was probably a good thing, as I would have been overwhelmed if they had all come home at once. At the time, they were ages nine through fifteen. The early months were spent reading everything I could get my hands on, while the kids worked out of workbooks from a popular Christian curricula company. The more I read, the more intrigued I was with unschooling. I hopped from email list to email list, seeking information and like minded individuals.

Our journey is just beginning, but we've come full circle. I made the big leap into unschooling in the fall of 1998, and put away all those expensive, colorful workbooks. The kids had to be constantly reminded to stay on task, and I knew that they were not retaining much of what they learned. But oh, how I loved those workbooks! They gave me such comfort. They brought me back to the days of my own early childhood.

Through the encouragement of several key individuals whom I had corresponded with by email, I completely revamped our homeschool program. This is truly funny to see myself write this as I sit here, as I have been "revamping" ever since. Unschooling is simply doing what works. Some would be horrified to hear that you use a text book, but if that is what your child thrives on and yearns to read, then that is where you should turn. Unschooling is tailoring each child's education to their unique learning styles. Unschooling has no rules, no boundaries and no time constraints. One of our four is a night owl, and does her best work at one in the morning. We allow for her peculiar school hours because this is what works.

I guess the best place to begin is at the beginning, so I will back up a bit, and share what has happened in our family, and our lives in the past five years. About five years ago, we were your average American family, kids in school, Mom and Dad both working. We had some extremely difficult times with a neighbor of ours, and I believe that was the impetus that pushed me right into the arms of Jesus. During my quest for some sort of peace in my heart, I found God, and was born again. He helped me to completely change my life. I had used curse words fluently since the second grade, but God worked through me to conquer that habit. But now we had a mother, trying her best to live a Godly life, yet all four of our children were raised in an ungodly home. None knew Christ, and they rolled their eyes and turned their backs at the mention of His name. My wonderful husband Michael, was a strayed Christian and tolerated my new love for Jesus with patience.

The Holy Spirit has moved in our family and done a tremendous work. A year ago, our oldest became Born Again, and a few months ago, my husband Michael opened his heart to God once more. The three youngest children are open to His word, but have not yet made a commitment. We pray that will happen soon. We know that with God, all things are possible, and we try to be patient.

At this point in time, our children are all involved in very different lifestyles. It is difficult to give an example of an "average" day in our household, as there are no average days. I will give you a brief summary of each of the children, and then try to sum things up so that they make some sense.

Our oldest daughter Angeli, who is 17 now, spent a semester deschooling, then started the dual enrollment/homeschooling program at the local community college. She thrives in a heavy academic environment, but detested the social aspects of the local high school. She carries a full course load, while earning high school as well as college credit. This gives her the freedom to tailor her own schedule around her various activities. She attends a local church where she was baptized a few months ago and attends the youth group there, as well as church services. During the week she has a daily private time. She also volunteers at the local hospital as a candy striper, or junior auxilian, as they now call them. She is in her eighth year of violin, and takes private lessons once a week, as well as performing with the local youth symphony orchestra. For fitness, she works out with weights three times a week, and takes karate classes twice a week. She has plans to transfer to Stetson University and become an English major, then enter the military where she wants to go to law school. Angeli's nickname is "The Rock" which refers to her strength of mind and morals. She is an amazing young lady who will go far in life.

Amber is now 15, and has turned her life around. She has pretty much left behind the social life with her public school peers and only sees one or two friends on occasion. She has made many new friends since coming home, most of them adults. She has great potential, and the moral direction she has received since coming home has made a world of difference.

Amber is our free spirit. She works on projects, which we do in composition notebooks, and in between projects she fills in time researching various people and places of interest. She has done major projects on the holocaust, Kahlil Gibran and Louis Comfort Tiffany. She has also become interested in the Greek Gods, and done quite a bit of reading in that area. Kahlil Gibran has reached her spiritual nature, where I could not, and opened her heart to the things in life that matter, the things in life that she cannot see. She owns most of his books, or has read them, and occasionally writes poetry when moved to do so.

Her math skills when she came home were poor. Though the public school had her at an Algebra-1 level, she had little understanding of the basics of math. We use the *Keys to...* series, and we are having her cover the basics again before moving on to Algebra. She works in her books on a near daily basis at whatever time she is moved to work in them and does however many pages she likes.

We help our children set goals, and one of Amber's goals is to follow her older sister's lead and finish high school at the community college. So, though we do not require a certain amount of math to be done, she knows that she must be able to take the entrance tests at the community college.

Amber is an avid surfer, and some mornings, if the surf is up, she will ride her bike or skateboard down to the beach for a two or three hour session. She hopes to start competing in local contests this year. She also works out at the local gym three times a week and takes karate twice weekly. Amber is an excellent typist, as is her older sister, thanks to Mavis Beacon and email! Amber keeps in touch with many other homeschoolers all over the country and has plans to meet one of them when his family comes to Florida for a visit.

During her free time, she goes to the library, skates and visits with friends. She baby-sits fairly regularly and now has a part-time weekend job bussing tables at a local restaurant. I pray for the Holy Spirit to give this child of mine some direction, because she will be unstoppable one day.

Amanda is 13 and the most social of my children. She has held on for dear life to her public school buddies and seems the most dependent on them for focus in her life. This is disturbing to us as parents, yet we are patient, as Amanda was the last of the four to come home. Amanda is a bright young lady with great leadership abilities. She is the most open of the three youngest children to accepting Christ as her Lord and Savior.

She enjoys having me read to her and is enthusiastic about the *Left Behind* series. She is also working on the *Keys to* ...series in Math, for the same reasons as Amber. Poor basics. She works on them whenever the spirit moves her, usually at about two in the morning! She also works on various notebook projects and has put in a tremendous amount of work on subjects like the Solar System, Jack the Ripper and Creative Writing.

She is currently working on a short story which is turning into a long story. Her typing and spelling skills have improved greatly since coming home from school. We point out grammar and spelling errors to the girls, but do not have them correct, as I enjoy seeing the improvement from month to month. Amanda also takes karate twice weekly and is beginning to show a real interest in the weapons class. She will begin weight training soon. Geography is one of Amanda's strong points and she initiated a contest between the siblings as to who could remember the states and capitals as well as identify states by shape only. They pretended they were on a game show and all three of them learned their capitals! Amanda also works well with the Carmen Sandiego CD ROM, and we occasionally play a geography board game called "Take off!" Amanda has also become interested in writing Bible verses, and is currently working on Proverbs. She baby-sits and plays Playstation in her free time. Amanda does not know what she wants to do with her life at this time, but she is on the road to success already, as she is discovering that learning can be fun and rewarding!

Adam is our 11 year old. He is very independent and self sufficient. Adam is a competitive surfer, who has been surfing since he was five, and competing since he was eight. He is currently unschooling in Costa Rica at Loma Del Mar, a Christian surf camp owned by some friends. This is his third trip by himself, and he thrives down there. He has learned so much from traveling out of the country and making friends with the people who live there.

Adam enjoys math and has been working out of Saxon, though we do not use it how it was intended to be used. We work to proficiency and then move on, only touching on past principles with one or two problems to keep him current. He works on book projects of his own, most of them centering around famous surfers, surfing spots and countries with good surf! He also has an encyclopedic knowledge of different countries and their most popular breaks. He recognizes famous surfers by their style and the location of a break just by the shape of the wave, without any identifying landmarks.

He has a developing interest in clouds and weather patterns, and can identify most cloud formations. He understands tides, wind patterns, and knows about sea life on the southeast coast of the US. He enjoys drawing and is fairly talented. Adam joins us in our geography games, and loves being read to, though not reading alone (unless it's surfing magazines). We read the Bible daily, as well as many other books. Fitness is taken care of in his surfing, as well as skateboarding, weight training and karate with his sisters.

Our goals as parents are to raise kids who know Jesus as their personal Lord and Savior, who love learning, who attack interests with a passion and succeed in whatever endeavors they choose. We would also hope that they learn discretion, and look for the godliness in people, and not judge people by the way they dress, the careers they've chosen or the money they make. We have gone beyond our previous aspirations for them all to become "rocket scientists." Now, we want them to find true happiness. We also hope to have taught them that freedom in life is choices. Choices in education, careers, family life and in all they do. I feel a sadness that I came to these realizations so late in our children's lives. I cannot turn back the clock and recapture all those precious years, but I can give my all to make sure that my children do not become "part of this world." For God tells us to remain apart from the world and this is a battle He can help us to win. I praise God in all that we do, and thank Him for leading us to homeschooling. It has brought our family, which was fragmenting at an alarming rate, back together to become a strong, close knit, loving unit.

A Long Road

by Lorrie Flem

We have traveled a long road in our homeschool journey. It began with me reading about and exploring almost every homeschool product that I heard about. Since I didn't want to make a mistake I needed to consider every product before making any final decisions.

After scaling the mountain of accumulated catalogs we settled down with a program for each subject, certain that our prayerful choices were the best, and life was good . . .for a while.

Then I began noticing things like, "Mom, do I have to do school?" instead of the precious happy compliance. Eventually, I realized that we were doing "school at home". Our homeschool was a miniaturization of public school, which I knew was a failure for my kids.

So it was back to the mountain of catalogs, though it was much smaller since I had already done so much weeding. This time I was sure that unit studies were the way to go. Now we could learn about the things that naturally interesting to them, while easily including the younger brother. We used a few programs to cover the basics and spent the rest of our days enjoying unit studies . . . for a while.

Then I began to hear someone gasping for air, someone was drowning. It was me! I couldn't keep up with the planning required for unit studies in addition to my other responsibilities. Since our trouble now was teacher prep time, we decided to do what we had never done before and buy a "canned" curriculum. After paying too much, we had a teacher's manual that told me what pages of which books to do so that when we were through we had completed a certain grade. The boys liked their new books and Mom could once again breathe freely . . . for a while.

If you are wondering if I am ever content, I held that same question. Was there even a homeschool curriculum for us that was written? What a shock to realize that, "No, indeed, there was not!" Even though I asked the Lord to bless each choice I made, unknowingly, I was leaving Him out of the decision making process. This was a humbling realization—yet I knew it was true.

After reading *The Homeschool Jumpstart Navigator* and *Wisdom's Way of Learning*, I was freed from the self-imposed doubts and began to understand that teaching is not a matter of me taking what I know and forcing it into children. The best way to learn is not for the children to remain passive while I teach. The author of *Wisdom's Way of Learning* says this causes the child to "lose interest in real learning and develop an appetite for all kinds of passive, entertaining media ... true education will occur as the student procures the knowledge for himself."

Does this mean I am not needed? No, I am a vital part of this. I must be involved in the learning process along with my children. I need to be involved in their lives and observant to what interests them while keeping as my primary concern the needs of their hearts. My genuine interest is essential to this process. My role is to train them in the necessities of life while watching for what they are naturally interested in. Their interests are no longer an "extra" to be looked into after we get through the academics. Instead, these interests have become the core of our school.

Establishing a daily routine that centers around your home and skills, talents, interests and resources at hand involves *active* training and discipline of the children to establish a peaceful godly home life. I must walk with the Spirit to achieve a teacher- and student-planned, goal-oriented, parent-lead purpose.

I mentioned two books that were the catalyst for change in our homeschool. *The Homeschool Jumpstart Navigator* is what made me aware that I needed to be re-educated. As the author of this book says, "Before a parent ever launches into setting up a curriculum for her child, she needs to go through a season of re-educating herself, allowing God time to 'transform her [ideas of education] by the renewing of her mind.'

As I was reading I felt the tugs of the Holy Spirit convicting me that she was right. I needed to begin by climbing out of the curriculum pit I had dug for us. I needed to stop depending on someone or some curriculum to tell me what to do next and to look to the Lord in order to see His vision for my children.

I became the student and began my re-education by following her suggestions. I read and took the recommended course of action, which is really one of *no* action. While I was waiting on the Lord, we went through a long dry spell in my children's creative ventures. I was horrified to realize that they seemed to have *no* interests or hobbies other than the few I had dreamt up for them. I found myself wondering, *would they ever show an unprompted interest in something?*

But God is faithful even though I am not: "but those who hope in the Lord will renew their strength" Isaiah 40:31. After about two months of beseeching the Lord for guidance and begging encouragement from my husband, our then 11-year-old, John casually asked me if he could get out his knife and carve something. After a few minutes I realized that he was initiating interest in something creative. Yippee!

He began to put out more carved figures than we had Ivory soap! On his own and without a book or Mom he was figuring out ways to improve upon them as he went along. He soon moved from carving to building his own designs of furniture from scrap wood. These pieces are among my most prized possessions today.

About this same time my 8-year-old, Levi, timidly asked if he could get the spider he had found outside and put it in a jar. Now this goes against my womanly instincts (bring a spider from outside *into* my house?). I was less than enthusiastic. However, I was trying to watch for signals from them to see what their interests were so . . . "Sure," I hesitantly said.

By now, all three boys and two girls were involved. After a few hours of intent observation intermingled with squeals of delight they were ready for more "research." In order to see if spiders fight with each other they needed to catch more. On their way back inside with 14 of these marvelous creatures there was an appalling crash as the jar hit the marble floor! I was quite proud of myself for calmly saying, "Was that the spider jar?"

Of course it was. I heard my four-year-old daughter, Dessaly, say, "I got three of them!" This was promptly followed by more shouts of "I gots." Then I heard the whispered comment, "Where is number 14? Mom won't like it if we don't find him."

I didn't need to know something in order for my children to learn it. I could just enjoy learning right at their side. What fun (well most of it!). My children were learning through discovery and were eager for more. We were ready for a new lifestyle. One that looks at everything, even spiders, as a learning experience.

There has been an even more exciting benefit. I found myself falling even more in love with my children as I watched their ideas flow from smiling lips and sparkling eyes. As we began to make booklets to record our learning we often became so engrossed that we had trouble limiting our "school" hours so that we have time to make dinner.

Looking back, my only regret is that I didn't read these books when I first started homeschooling. We would have had a much more enjoyable journey and have many more dollars in the bank! If you are just beginning or not delighting in your homeschool, don't make this same mistake. Set aside your scope and sequence charts and follow God's leading instead of "your own understanding" and let Him "make your paths straight."

Our Family Unschool

by Kristy Kronz

My husband and I started researching homeschooling after the birth of our first son Josia. The thought of someday relinquishing our role as the major influence in our child's life seemed absurd. School is not an option for us; not because of its low standards, peer influences or liberal philosophies, but because of the limitations it imposes. We want more for our kids ...and boy, have we gotten it! Our kids are still quite young, but because we consider our children's education as beginning at birth, we feel like veterans!

The most important aspect of our family's unschooling involves the opportunities we have provided and nurtured within our family. Much to the chagrin of many (so much so that we have stopped telling people), we provided many intellectual stimuli for our boys when they were infants and toddlers. This included books, books and more books! Also we invested in large flashcards showing and giving facts about insects, birds, sea life, butterflies, farm animals, composers, flowers, great works of art, trees and so on. My kids were sponges! They didn't want to sing Twinkle, Twinkle little star again. They wanted to learn, to hear new words, to see vibrant pictures. I remember Isaac barely able to crawl, coming as fast as his chubby little legs could bring him just at the simple word, flashcards.

These tools have been invaluable to us in our nature walks as we label everything... "Look at the swallow tail butterfly among the Bog Goldenrod." I even remember walking in the city and passing a sign advertising an orchestral performance. The picture above the advertisement was of Schubert. Josia recognized the picture immediately, "There's Schubert, Mommy," he exclaimed proudly. He was barely three.

Unschooling isn't a style of teaching, or not teaching, it's a lifestyle which has afforded us the luxury of incorporating our faith into every aspect of our day. We begin our day with breakfast and Christian radio. Since we have made the personal choice to not watch television, the radio is where we turn for news, weather and inspirational words to start our day. Next we kneel at our bench for Prayer ... for our church and pastors, friends, family and for ourselves. Each day we have assigned a particular request. We always end with the Lords Prayer. Sometimes I play the piano or organ and sing a hymn. I'm determined that they hear the great hymns even though they aren't played in our contemporary church service.

From here our day is our own and completely up for grabs. We play, we bake, we work on the computer and often listen to Spanish over lunch. We love to go for nature walks and draw in our nature notebooks then come home and look up things in the encyclopedia, which leads to other lessons. We read, read and read some more. We play Bible stories and race to see who can memorize a piece of scripture the fastest. We play instruments, (we have a guitar, piano, a recorder and a huge assortment of little instruments) we sing, dance and giggle a lot. Sometimes I make Josia write words, perhaps even short sentences. Usually he balks at this, but I think it's important and so I call it learning time. It's one of my failures as an unschooler... oh well, I'm allowed.

In the Fall and Winter we have a daily ritual of hot cocoa with whipped cream and sprinkles. This is when we do our best reading, particularly biographies about composers, great artists, historical figures or scientists. We might do science experiments, play with cuisenaire rods or watch educational videos. We might sing church camp songs while we swing in the backyard. If the moon is visible, Josiah will want the telescope up on his fort where he can explore the craters and sight a bird's nest in the process.

We regularly answer questions from our discoveries in the encyclopedias and dictionaries. Josiah goes to bed "reading" his latest books on the revolutionary war. I've never limited him to the number or type of books he picks out at the library. His two month long fascination with the fact and heroes of the revolutionary war has led him to looking at countless 4th and 5th grade level books on the subject. Twice we went to Fort McHenry to learn about the battle of Baltimore. These experiences provide an incredible learning opportunity for us all and are so much more meaningful when they stem from our own interests.

For us living is learning. My son's fascination with flight has only been fueled by trips to Kitty Hawk, The national Museum of Air and Space and Fairchild Air force base. The music of Tchaikovsky came to life as we watched our local community college perform *The Nutcracker*. When construction equipment was his passion we'd make a point to stop at construction sites. Josiah's Grandpa even arranged for him to take a bulldozer ride in the wilderness of Eastern Washington.

The most wonderful thing is that we can incorporate God into all this learning. We can leave if the subject matter is inappropriate. We can pray when life becomes frustrating or fearful. Most importantly, we are together so that all of life's other distractions seem boring compared to the fun we create as a family. God is there with us as we identify plants and trees, as we walk and sing, as we pray before our field trips and as we rest in the safety of his love. What a gift this has been. Isn't this what God intended when we became a family?

Our Journey into Unschooling

by Michele Hastings

When I met my husband 10 years ago, I hadn't even heard of homeschooling. I had seen a book about it on his bookshelf, but assumed it had something to do with his nephew who had Williams Syndrome. Then, when our first son was just a toddler, Ted attended a homeschooling information night and determined in his heart to have both of our kids home-educated. Well, I fought this idea tooth and nail, thinking that this went way beyond the "call of duty" as a parent! When Tymon was about three, Ted invited me to come to a homeschooling convention that was being held at a church in our city and I consented. I'd held this idea that homeschoolers were kerchiefwearing, bread-baking, earth-mommas, which I was not! Upon participating in the classes, I still had serious doubts about me being able to do this. I'd entertained fantasies about walking my first-born to school, along with my younger son and pushing a stroller with our yet-to-be-born child in it. Then, once all our kids were in school, I'd have some time to myself to maintain our home, do aerobics and maybe take up painting again! This was just not fitting in to my plan!

Near the end of the conference, I was surprised by a speaker named Jacki Knight. I could really relate to her. She was colorful and flamboyant and I was extremely impressed by her testimony of how homeschooling had drawn her family closer together. She went into the personality styles of individual family members and I really listened to what she had to say. I left that day, although being overwhelmed with the many curriculum choices, feeling that maybe, just maybe, God *was* calling us into this lifestyle choice.

That was the beginning of my soul-searching as I began to research all of our options. We discussed the pros and cons of public school, separate school, French Immersion and Christian school. Homeschooling began to look better and better! Then I proceeded to read the many available books at the libraries about homeschooling, as well as whatever magazines I could get my hands on.

I had envisioned homeschooling as "school at home", scheduling in times for schooling and housework, errands etc. Some of the books and magazines I'd read seemed to confirm this and I wrote and rewrote imaginary schedules, trying to come up with the most efficient way to go about this.

I attended another information night, put on by our Provincial Homeschooling Association, and drilled the people sitting on the panel with question after question. They kept on telling me to relax, as we didn't even have to register our five year old until he was about to turn seven. They reassured me that we had plenty of time to find our way before we were actually accountable to the school board. Anxiety ridden, we began our Kindergarten year with fear and trepidation!

Another thing I had done to "put to rest" the questions and fears I had about socialization, was to call the 24-hour phone line that the local support group provided, to hear what types of activities would be offered for them to participate in. I got excited when I heard about all the wonderful activities that they could be involved with!

Regretfully, things didn't go as planned when my son and I began to sit down each day to do school. He didn't seem to be interested in doing the things that other Kindergarten kids were supposed to do, according to the scope-and-sequences that I'd poured over in my research! Although he loved being read to, which we'd done together since his birth, he had no desire to actually learn letters. He also hated writing numbers, although he loved to color and draw pictures! It was so frustrating for me to see him color in with extravagant detail the parrots on the math page, instead of just circling them to "count" the number of parrots in the picture.

I continued to educate myself about homeschooling and discovered that there were many different styles of homeschooling. As we proceeded along our journey of home-education , I realized that we seemed to be fitting into three of the five common "approaches" which were:

- The Living Books and Life Experiences or Charlotte Mason Approach which consisted of involving our children in real-life situations and giving them ample time to play and create.
- The Unit Study Approach which blends all subjects together along common themes.
- The Unschooling Approach which concludes that children have an innate desire to learn and a curiosity that drives them to learn what they need to know when they need to know it, according to John Holt who wrote *Learning All the Time*.

I also read books by Dr. Raymond and Dorothy Moore like; *The Successful Homeschool Family Handbook, Better Late Than Early* and *School Can Wait*. These grandparents of homeschooling believed that academics shouldn't even be introduced until between the ages of eight and twelve!

Even then, there should be a "balance" between academics, work and service.

One of the best resources, that I wished I'd gotten a hold of earlier, was a catalog put out by Elijah Company. In it were the teaching approaches, along with resources that fit with each approach. Reading that book first would have saved me a lot of confusion.

As I read these books, one would lead me to the next. Meanwhile, our school-at-home evolved into a more relaxed pattern of reading books that the boys and I both picked out according to their interests, playing board games and computer games and doing projects that inspired the boys' curiosity. We also performed science experiments along with another homeschooling family we'd become close with. There were also daily chores and errands to be done and often tours and field trips, alone as a family, or with the social group. We made the most of "teachable moments" as we went along with our daily routines. I'd been told by fellow homeschoolers that God is a God of order and not of chaos and therefore unschooling wasn't very "Christian" in it's approach. No one else that I knew, who were Christians, was doing what we were doing, yet we strongly believed that we were walking along in God's plan for us.

With three years, many books and a few conventions under our belts, (all very supportive of the unschooling method) we, in faith, proceed each day to move in whatever direction God directs us. Because my older son has now turned eight, we may structure the basics a bit more come fall. I also see the need for more service in our kids' lives. I am very confident that by following our kids' interests, going at their own pace, incorporating their unique learning styles into all we do and using as many practical life experiences as we can, both boys are benefiting while discovering who God created them to be. Their creativity, depth of knowledge and breadth of knowledge is far beyond what I could have imagined. Their enthusiasm for learning is still intact and we have the close relationship that I'd hoped for. If they were in school they probably would read and write better than they presently do, and they'd probably have their times-table memorized. They also might be more disciplined than they are right now. However, they might hate school, they might not have the understanding of the concepts they have now, and the discipline wouldn't necessarily be self discipline. My desire is to see them develop inward motivation, rather than to adhere to external rewards and punishment.

So we're content "plugging along." We seek God's will each step of the way while keeping in mind our vision for the future. We envision the boys involved in volunteer, apprentice and entrepreneurial activities as teenagers then moving into a trade or being self-employed as adults. If university is the means to whatever end they each have in mind, I'm confident that whatever their goals are, they will attain it.

Unschooling Unchristian?

by James Muncy

Many homeschoolers are teaching their children through an approach called unschooling. As the name implies, it is opposite to all that traditional schools do. Some people believe that unschooling is unchristian. I don't think so. Let me explain why.

When people ask me what unschooling is, I tell them that it is where we "create a learning rich environment and then let the kids go." Kids are naturally curious. I believe God made them that way. Let kids loose and they will rush headlong into learning.

We don't need to do anything to get children excited about learning. The only reason any child doesn't see learning as pure joy is because we make it a miserable experience. We take a child who was made to be active and tell him to sit for six hours in the name of learning. Then we wonder why he doesn't like to learn. It's like taking ice cream, pouring used motor oil on top of it, and wondering why a child doesn't like ice cream.

Around our home, our learning environment consists of three components. First, we have a compulsory component. We are not pure unschoolers because we do expect and ensure that our children do learn certain things. But this is the smallest part of our educational experience. We only do this in areas where the child might not see the educational value before the learning experience. Perhaps I am of little faith, but I can't see our children memorizing their multiplication tables "just for fun."

Second, there is an environmental component. We create a learning rich environment. Everything in our home has educational value. Some of what we have fosters creativity. Other materials present facts. There are shelves and shelves of books. We have many educational CDs for the computer. Our walls have posters and maps. Arts and crafts supplies abound (I know, I trip over them all the time). We have one whole closet that is nothing but supplies needed for science experiments. We don't need to hold constant watch over our children to get them to learn. We just let them do whatever they can find to do. We know it will have educational value.

Third, we have a social component. We are active participants with our children in the educational experience. Education is what we do *with* our children and not what we do *to* our children. Our children like to read because mom and dad like to read. Our children like math because mom and dad like math. Our children discuss geography because mom and dad discuss geography. Our children like science because mom and dad find science interesting. Kids love to be "part of the action" and, around our house, the action is learning.

Unschooling emphasizes the second and third of these components. We can argue about whether or not the compulsory component is necessary. I don't see a clear Biblical mandate that it either is or is not. But even if the compulsory component is important, the environmental and social components are clearly superior in helping our children learn. Children will keep their love for learning alive when they are having fun learning what they have chosen to learn. They will learn more when they are learning what interests them. As the ancient proverb states, when the student is ready, the teacher will appear. And, regardless of what our popular culture proclaims, loving parents are still the most influential people in children's lives. If we are excited about learning, our children will be excited too.

So, we have three components of a learning system. I acknowledge that all three components may be necessary. But I also recognize that two of the components are more important, more effective, and more fun than the other one. Put quite simply, there are two superior components and one inferior component. Is there Christian virtue in emphasizing the inferior component over the superior two? Are we doing what the Bible commands when we force our children to do something they hate when, with a little creativity, we could make it enjoyable for them?

Not long ago I went to the doctor for some tests. No treatment was needed, but let's say it was. One form of treatment meant drinking a glass of liquid that tasted much like a chocolate milkshake. A second form of treatment meant receiving a nice back massage from my wife. The third treatment would require surgery and weeks of painful recovery. Then my doctor tells me that he is prescribing the surgery. I ask why? Is it more effective? "No, actually it is less effective."

"Then why are you prescribing the surgery?" I hypothetically demanded.

"See, I am a Christian," he replies. "Even though the other two treatments are more effective, they are also more enjoyable. They won't provide you the opportunity to learn to deal with pain. So I am prescribing the painful surgery. You may not get well, but you will learn to deal with pain."

What would I do? I would quickly find another doctor. I would tell all my friends to avoid him too. "Don't go near him. He wants me to do the most painful thing even when enjoyable treatments are more effective. And he says he is doing so because he is a Christian. He isn't a Christian. He's a madman."

I don't think parents who choose a structured learning environment are unchristian. I just hope they do so because they believe, mistakenly in my opinion, that they provide the most effective learning environment. I respect their Christian faith, even if we disagree on educational philosophy. But if we subject our child to an inferior pedagogy in the absence of a clear Biblical mandate simply because it is the Christian thing to do, we need to rethink our concept of Christian parenting. It is not *despite* being Christians that we've incorporated many of the ideas of unschooling into our homeschooling experience. We do so because we believe that they are more consistent with Biblical parenting as we see it. It is not only possible to be a Christian unschooler. Christians homeschoolers should feel obligated to investigate the advantages of an unstructured learning environment and consider letting more and more of a child's direction be determined by creating a learning rich environment and providing strong parental role models. The loving and therefore Christian thing to do, is to make coercion a last resort.

The How and Why of our Homeschool

by Patricia Moon

My husband Joseph and I have been married for almost seven years. I spent the first years of our marriage attending college, while Joe held a full-time job as a machinist. I tried my hand at selling real estate for a few years, until we bought our home in the woods. Then I made calls from home for a charity. I am now a full-time stay-at-home mom. I am pursuing my ambition to be a published writer, while homeschooling our children.

Both Sara (12), and Jon (10) , were in a co-op daycare at the college I attended. I ran between classes, nursing Jon and playing with them both. When Sara was four, I started visiting local kindergartens to see what they were like. I remembered feeling overwhelmed by the classrooms; the walls, windows, doors and even ceilings were filled with "educational" charts and the like. It seemed chaotic to me. The teachers were nice, but rather condescending to the children. My impression was that they were trying to pack as much information into those young brains as quickly as possible. I went home feeling more than a little dazed.

At that time I was divorced and a single mom, trying to figure out how I could possibly find a job after college without putting my children in a regular daycare. I wanted to be part of their lives. From my classroom visits, I discovered that I really didn't want Sara to go to public school. The more I thought about it the more I knew that was not an option for us. I began researching the many alternatives to public school. In every situation, whether daycare or school, it felt like the adults were herding mindless cattle, while also trying to cram those minds with information. It just didn't feel right.

So many things were limited for me during that period--time, money and sleep. However, I did have an incredible circle of support from family and friends. I also had determination. I knew I wasn't going to get a second chance to do what I felt was right for my children.

When Joseph came into our lives, many of the pressures eased up. It was good to have someone to share the joys and the burdens of parenting. Between the two of us, we were able to get Sara into a kindergarten class in a small private school that felt right. The classroom was quiet, calm and dimly lit. A beautiful mural, painted in pastels, covered one entire wall. The room was decorated with branches, rocks, shells and other items from nature. There were many capes and crowns and other materials for the make-believe world of play. Lunch was eaten in the classroom and the children participated in making and serving snacks, as well as clean- up. It was their special place. There were music, stories, puppet plays, art and a garden out back. The children had fun, but there was also a sense of reverence. I wanted to move in, but they wouldn't let me.

Jon stayed with family, friends and sometimes home daycares, while Joe, Sara and I went to work and school. Jon and I also spent a lot of time at Sara's school that year because I was running the school store for a partial scholarship for Sara's tuition.

The next year Jon attended the preschool at Sara's school. The hardship was paying the tuition and traveling 40 minutes, twice a day. Those hardships kept us from enrolling Sara in the second grade and Jon in kindergarten. By this time we lived in a rural community, and conveniently, one block from the Primary school. The time and money we would save was a big draw, so we enrolled Sara in the public school. That lasted all of three months, then she was back to her private school. She spent third grade there, on a part-time basis, and we were homeschooling both children. Until this year, we spent every August and September trying to decide where the children would go to school. Now there is no question, we will homeschool, of course!

I suppose we would be called natural learners because we don't use one curriculum. I gather bits and pieces of the 3 R's and sometimes we "play" school. Mostly we draw from our interests and follow where they lead.

"Sure you can make that recipe, but we'll have to learn a bit about fractions..."

"Sure, you can join Scouts, but you'll have to practice your reading skills to work in the book..."

"Yes, we can build that, but you'll have to learn to use a tape measure and those tools..."

The children have opened their own savings accounts, apprenticed with several people who own businesses that they were interested in, and help with shopping and all family errands. We write and publish a community newsletter and they helped when I delivered real estate flyers for a part-time business. They both write stories and poetry. They participate in some group sports and we have a tutor who comes to the house for piano and Spanish lessons. We haven't watched television in about seven years. We do rent movies once in a while and we all read the newspaper and talk about current events. We do some field trips with our family, homeschool groups and public school groups. The children haul, chop and stack wood. They do dishes and laundry and both love to cook. We garden and explore our woods. They know a lot about almost every plant, animal and bird living in our area. Sara and Jon are active members of the community, both through their church and the community hall.

The reasons for homeschooling are not as cut and dried for us as they are for many homeschoolers that we know. I would suppose that the long and short of it is that we want to provide our children with a wider experience than they would get in a public or private school. We want them to see and live and question the world without following a generally prescribed formula. We do not homeschool out of fear, yet we are aware of the negatives in public school, and are glad to miss out on some of those negatives. We do not homeschool in order to mold our children to our own beliefs, although we know that they will probably lean our way as they explore a wide world of beliefs. These are our children, and it has never felt right to send them off to learn about the world from adult strangers and other children.

Chapter Eleven

A Day in Our Life

I love writing about our days. Every time I write about one of our days, I am encouraged by the amount of learning that goes on that makes an ordinary day, extraordinary. As I write this my daughter is at the kitchen table with a friend. They are drawing, painting and creating. While they do this they're discussing having an art show and selling their work at the top of the street. My daughter has just learned to draw three dimensionally and she is sure that people will now wish to purchase her art. Questions are popping up such as, "How much should we charge?" "What should we buy with the money?" "Should we advertise?" I smile as they discuss these questions, watching their thinking and learning processes.

My son is out on the boat with his father as they fish for the elusive Chinook Salmon. During this time he will learn more about the river, the habits of salmon and boating, than I could ever teach him at home. I have never met an unschooler whose days could be classified as typical. There is a rhythm to many unschooler's days, but rarely could they be called typical. Each day the Lord has something new to teach us or show us.

How does your day look? As an exercise in encouragement, I recommend trying to write about a day in your home. Be aware of the possibilities, of the learning that goes on without it being directed. The following essays are typical days in the lives of unschoolers who admit that there are no typical days.

Our Own Paths

by Meg Chorpinning

It seems that "Christian" and "unschooling" are terms that are not permitted to be used together. To be committed to the Lord and to homeschool has become synonymous with desks, flags, workbooks and a strictly scheduled day. When I shared with other Moms in my Christian homeschool support group that I don't use a curriculum and I was very relaxed in my homeschool approach (it was too difficult to actually use the word unschooling), I was met with amazement. It seems to curriculum-dependent homeschoolers to be an act of great daring to allow learning to occur naturally. But as often as I hear, "I couldn't do that." I've heard just as many times, "I wish I could do that."

We are called by our Lord Jesus not to be conformed to this world, but to be transformed. Why would we want to conform to the human institution of public school? Simply because that's the way it's done in American culture isn't a good enough reason. It's also not a transforming work to add the Bible and prayer to a public school imitation and consider that what we're now doing is the Christian way.

Mary Hood says it best in her book, *The Joyful Homeschooler* "I'm convinced that God never called any of us to set up miniature institutions for our children. He wants us to go back to his original plan for the family and be the best parents we can be ... God did not create schools. He placed us in families... God's best scenario was the one he gave us to begin with: a circle of parents and children, working, learning and growing together."

So in our family, we do not have a set school day with desks and textbooks and emphasis on grade levels. We attempt to live out the philosophy that all of life is learning. My children are young, Faith is seven and David is six. They have always been educated at home and so far, have expressed no desire to go to school like the other kids on our street. I believe that even at this age, they understand that school would certainly limit their freedom. For that is what they have the most of right now—free time. Free time for David to build countless Lego creations, dig in the dirt and swing in the backyard. Time for Faith to read, play the piano or follow me around the kitchen while I work.

Before Dad goes off to work each day, we read the Bible, pray and practice memorizing scriptures as a family. We always have a chapter book in progress that I read aloud, (some of our favorite authors are Laura Ingalls Wilder, Astrid Lindgrin and Roald Dahl). Faith spends a little bit of time every day doing some math, (I use Miquon for guidance) and reading and writing her pen-pals. I do very relaxed unit studies that I make up myself, raiding the library for books to read aloud and ideas for craft projects and hands-on activities. Last year we learned about maps, pilgrims, birds, pioneers, caves and Australia. We have memberships to the state historical society, the zoo and the science center and we get our money's worth. Sometimes I think I homeschool because I can't stand to see my children stuck inside on a beautiful spring day. We make leaf collections, collect insects to watch, play in creeks and hike nature trails. On bad weather days we play games, do puzzles, use the computer, sew and bake. Faith and David make things with Dad in the workshop and help with projects around our old house. Through our church, we regularly visit some of our elderly shut-ins and we help to serve breakfast to the homeless on Sunday mornings.

We don't watch television except for the Lawrence Welk show on Saturday evening on our public television station, (at our children's insistence—I'm not kidding!) and occasional videos. My husband and I do not watch television and it helps that the TV is in the basement and not sitting as an idol in the living room. We have created a literate household with plenty of books and magazines and regular trips to the library.

What about socialization? Faith and David go to Sunday school and take classes at our local recreation center. They play with the neighborhood children, so much so that I am thankful when summer is over and the other children go back to school. They don't appear to, in any way, be incapable of making friends just because they're not in school. I have been part of a support group for the last two years, but as most of the members are curriculum users, I have found it to be of little support to me. So, I have been praying for some other like-minded homeschoolers.

As I watch my children learn and grow, I know that they are happier than they would be if they were in school. They have the time to learn at their own pace and in their own style. Whenever I feel pressured to "teach" I remember that my goals are not first and foremost academic but spiritual. We have chosen to unschool because we believe that it is educationally best for our children, not because of a desire to withdraw them from this world. As we believe that all life is learning so all life is to be redeemed and all aspects of our life to be brought under the Lordship of Jesus Christ. Instead of "teachers" we strive to be disciples of our children in their hearts and minds. I believe God will honor our efforts to raise our children to follow him.

A Working Unschool

by Nancy Rusk

My son is six-years-old and just finished the kindergarten year. We homeschooled him at my office. I work full-time and I own my own insurance agency. My son came with me to work and that's where we unschooled.

I set aside a bookcase in the back for Ben's stuff. We had some strict rules which did have to be followed for the whole thing to work: Ben could speak politely and ask questions while I was with a customer, but he was not to interrupt. No screaming inside (he spent afternoons outside at the day care center he's attended part-time since he was two and started preschool).

It worked well for us. Educationally, he followed his interests—ocean animals, the Bible and learning to read among his top choices. As a family, we were definitely enriched by the closeness. I didn't like the fact that he was in the day care center, and if a similar situation is ever necessary again I will make other choices for him. I found that the daycare center had a "lowest common denominator" mentality among the kids there and he didn't understand the cruelty and the meanness he witnessed. I will continue the homeschooling at home at this time, because his interests are greater and home will give us more outlets for them.

I suspect Christian unschoolers get it from both ends—from the usual "But what do you do for socialization?" questions from those who don't know about or agree with homeschool and also questions from more traditional homeschoolers. I have sensed disapproval from other Christians about our unschooling—comments about God valuing order, about how critically important it is to teach Ben various doctrines and catechisms, about how he'll be "behind." This is all fine and dandy, and I do believe in order and a solid doctrinal foundation. However, I also see that unschooling has done exactly what I believe God wanted it to do in my family. I see much stronger evidence of the fruits of the Spirit in me and in my family—more love, more gentleness with one another, more peace and kindness. I also see that God uses unschooling to give me the opportunity to show my son that Christianity is a joyful, incredible way of living—there is *nothing* better than serving Jesus Christ! Seeing me at work has given him an understanding of the work world as a mission field, yes, we pray for the customers and yes, we witness to them when God opens the door. God is so good to have given us this time together to do just that!

We often times had some interesting encounters with curious customers.

"Where do you go to school?" The nice customer asked my son.

"Here at the office," Benjamin answered honestly.

The lady smiled down at him. "You're sick today? Is that why you're not at school?"

Never one to shy away from confrontation, my son explained, "No, I'm not sick. I go to school at the office."

The customer looked at me for help, but I just nodded and smiled. "He's homeschooled,"

"Office schooled," Ben corrected. At five, he was a very precise child. And he was telling the truth: during Ben's kindergarten year he shared an insurance office with his mother. He spent his mornings learning and his afternoons at "after-school care" at a nearby daycare center.

As a new homeschooler, I came to the task armed with little else other than a fierce love for my son, a strong enjoyment of our time together and a burning desire to do God's will by homeschooling. When we first considered homeschooling, the autumn before Ben was to start kindergarten, it seemed completely out of reach. I worked full time at a busy insurance office. Having Ben with me at the office was nothing new, however. Throughout preschool he attended classes where I picked him up around two o'clock, and he spent afternoons with me at the office. I'm self-employed, and it worked reasonably well because my employees could run the office during the afternoon while I worked on paperwork in the back room with Ben "keeping me company." I purposely scheduled my days to do the tough stuff in the mornings when Ben was away and saved the tasks that didn't require my full attention for the afternoons. But homeschooling? Being completely responsible for my son's education? I couldn't see how it could possibly work. And yet...God kept the desire to homeschool alive.

In the end, God worked it all out in a typically awesome God way. Four months before Ben was to start kindergarten, I was approached with the opportunity to purchase a second office. I cheerfully explained to the man who offered me the opportunity that I had no money and no qualified manager for the second location. God had other plans, though, and during the next thirty days He worked out the details. The second office was smaller, quieter and closer to home. With a new office manager installed at the busier, more established office, I could homeschool Ben at the smaller, quieter one.

We quickly worked out the routine and the ground rules. Morning time was quiet at the new office and so we spent our mornings together. I learned quickly that my son loved hearing stories, and so I read for hour after hour, all the wonderful books I loved when I was young: *Ramona the*

Pest, Charlie and the Chocolate Factory, The Wizard of Oz. I found some new favorites, too: the original *Alice in Wonderland* (not the Disney version), *Stuart Little* and the *Narnia* books. We also read about anything and everything that interested Ben, including snakes, hurricanes, earthquakes, volcanoes, animals of all shapes and sizes...you name it, we read it. We played games for math: Junior Monopoly, Dominos, Chutes and Ladders. Ben started reading about halfway through the school year and he took off from there. (A year later, he reads on about a third grade level. Sorry, I just had to brag!)

There were a few frustrations, to be sure. There were times when I had to remind him that I was working with a customer. Each customer took only about fifteen minutes, but sometimes Ben didn't like to wait for my attention. Most of the customers were warmly enthusiastic about the whole thing. I'll never forget the way one elderly gentleman finished his insurance transaction and then spent twenty minutes sitting on the floor drawing pictures and explaining "perspective" to my attentive son. The main comment I heard frequently was a wistful "Wow...I sure wish I could do that at my job..."

This year, God's changed things around a little bit. Now I have excellent assistance in both my offices and so I'm able to be home with my son in the mornings. In the afternoon, Ben still attends "after-school care" and I cram eight hours of work into four, visiting both offices and supervising my employees.

Many, many customers from my original office ask about my son. They usually reminisce, "I remember when you were pregnant with him," or "I remember when he was a baby and you wrote up my insurance with him in his playpen next to you." Now when I visit the second office my customers ask, "Where's your little boy? I wanted to say hi to him."

I'm grateful to God that we were able to "color outside the lines" during Ben's kindergarten year. I'm also grateful that God opened all the doors at just the right times for our family to grow closer to one another and to Him.

Chapter Twelve

Lessons and Learning

Unschooling success stories thrill my heart and encourage me to continue on my family's chosen path. There are many such stories, children who have followed their interests with more success than anyone, including their parents, could have imagined. Or maybe stories of children suddenly understanding something they were determined to understand on their own terms. Most unschoolers have these stories, the interest that turned into a passion, the questions that became the family's month long project. Each story is unique to the family or the child, but it is also the ripe promise of what is possible for each of us.

As we share these stories with one another, we are giving the gift of encouragement, bolstering our faith in our Lord, our educational practices and our choices. Children learn in a multitude of different ways, hearing accounts of these differences can help us to accept our children's unique way of understanding their world.

The following essays all show how distinctive styles of unschooling happen and the wonderful results that follow.

Behind the Mask: What the Phantom of the Opera Taught Us

by Amy Hollingsworth

The great thing about following your child's interests is that they are infinitely more interesting than anything you could dream up on your own. I'm not exactly the spontaneous type. I like my ducks in a row—a really, really straight row. The only thing I like better than making a list is crossing things off that list. But what I've found is that if I rein in my compulsiveness a bit, my children lead me to heights my list would never permit me to go. That's how our love affair with the Phantom of the Opera began.

It was a casual affair at first. My son Jonathan, then six, was introduced to the infamous Opera Ghost through PBS' "Wishbone." Since all I knew about the story was that there was a mask involved, we searched for more information on the Internet. We tapped into a musical gallery and spent the afternoon listening to a sampling from Andrew Lloyd Webber's Broadway production. I must admit, it was amusing to watch my son belt out, "Sing, my Angel of Music!" as my four-year-old daughter responded at fever pitch and swooned as Christine.

That appeased us for a while. But when my mother sent us a CD featuring highlights from the musical, the spark was again ignited. There were days when every member of our household was milling around either humming or singing out, "The Phantom of the Opera is there . . . inside my mind." Since he was, evidently, still there inside our minds, we threw ourselves headfirst into the high society life of Paris in the late 1800's. We began reading Gaston Leroux's 1911 novel *The Phantom of the Opera*, which started the whole craze. (I was as surprised as anyone that Lon Chaney's cinematic feat as the Phantom was based on the novel, not the other way around.) Through Leroux, we discovered that the sad saga of the Phantom, the outcast who lived beneath the Paris Opera House hiding his disfigured face, was based on actual events. We learned that he was not a monster, but a genius, a musical prodigy, an accomplished inventor. We wrung our hands over his unrequited love for opera ingenue Christine Daae, to whom he appeared as an Angel of Music. We despaired over his thoughtless taking of lives, at the same time recalling that he had lived as a caged animal in a circus freak show. We cried when we read that his mother had rejected him, a fact movingly expressed in the musical: "This face, which earned a mother's fear and loathing; a mask, my first unfeeling scrap of clothing." And then came the climax, when the Phantom's mask fell away and Christine dissolved years of pain with an act of kindness even his mother had refused him, a kiss.

It became a lesson indelibly etched in our hearts, a poignant reminder to think twice about playground taunts and unkind words.

Of course we learned other lessons as well. We discovered what life was like in Paris in the 1880's. We received our first introduction to the opera. We learned about architecture and the construction of the Paris Opera House, how its 17 stories, numerous trap doors and underground lake set the stage for the Phantom's antics. We learned what a "portcullis" was, which came in handy once we backtracked from the 19th century to the Middle Ages. We pored over the libretto of the Broadway musical, deciphering the metaphors and relishing in the poetic quality of the lyrics. We listened circumspectly to the "Music of the Night." I guess for something that wasn't on my list, it proved to be a pretty rich educational experience.

Since we had spent so much time getting to know the Phantom, it seemed only fitting that we meet him in person. We had learned late in the year that the musical was coming to a nearby city the following spring. With tickets in hand, my son and I made the two-hour trek in the rain to the theatre, conveniently located in the middle of a bustling and unfamiliar downtown. We drove around in circles trying to find an empty parking spot. We raced in the freezing rain to the crowded hall where we were to finally meet the man who had become our friend. We made it to our seats with only seconds to spare, due in part to my son's excitement, which required two trips to the bathroom. With a nod from the conductor, the curtain rose, the chandelier crackled and the show came alive. Jonathan and I huddled together, whispering our impressions. We peered through binoculars to look at costumes, then closed our eyes to fully absorb the musical splendor of it all. Much too quickly we were transported to the final scene, where the Phantom stood alone in his underground labyrinth, forsaken by his true love and hounded by a mob thirsty for retribution. As he softly sang what had become his life's sad anthem, "Masquerade, paper faces on parade; Masquerade, hide your face so the world can never find you," a single tear streamed down my son's face. In that moment I knew that no child is ever too young to tap into the emotions of complex individuals, to be drawn into and completely lost within a world of music and mystery. I also knew that none of my careful planning could have engendered such a response. In an attempt to satisfy my son's curiosity, we had unmasked the Phantom, and in the process, the scales had fallen from my eyes as well.

So What About Prepared Curriculum?

by Barb Shelton

And now we come to "The Million Dollar Question," meaning, if I had a dollar for every time I've been asked this, I'd be a millionaire. Okay, maybe not quite, but close. Here's the whole question as I generally hear it: *So what do you think about prepared curriculum? I mean, like going with a whole program of textbooks and workbooks for all the subjects? Can't it be "one option" for people who aren't as creative as others?*

The first thing I need to tell you before I give you my opinion is that I am very biased! Having homeschooled for 16 years now, and having had contact with hundreds of homeschoolers via my writing, speaking around the country, the Home-Based Education Course I teach, and the support groups I've been involved in, I have just seen too much to have anything but a biased view of any workbook-oriented approach to homeschooling.

We have somehow gotten this view that "education" is filling our kids' minds with facts and information. While certainly part of the picture, that is not what true education is. In my opinion. true education involves cooperating with God in preparing them "for the works He prepared for them to walk in," allowing time for the stuff God breathed in them to come to life while facilitating their thinking process and building character. This is why we are hearing so much about employers who are frustrated with the workforce that traditional school systems are producing. The schools are not producing "educated people" but rather "schooled" kids whose minds are only "puffed up with knowledge." Even knowledge from a Christian perspective "puffeth up" when the character has not been trained. This is *not* best done by a workbook on "Character Training." but within the context of a lifestyle where learning is a common, everyday occurrence.

You wouldn't believe the stack of letters I have received from home school moms who have been homeschooling for ten, even twelve years, and have written to me, some even in tears, frustrated over having tried the work-textbook approach for many years, only to now have nothing but burnt-out kids who hate learning and have retained very little of it anyway. They are overjoyed to have found the lifestyle of learning approach, but say "I can't tell you how much I wish I could go back and do it this way right from the start!" Letter after letter say the very same thing! Almost every one of them also says, "You have put into words what I felt God was saying, but could never figure it out!"

There is still a place, I believe, for using some prepared curriculum, sometimes when first starting and sometimes later on for selected subjects. But I have seen so many homeschoolers use it for their entire curriculum and I have never seen one bit of good fruit come from it–especially not the fruit the parents themselves were striving for. There's so much to be gained from real life experiences" and real books. (Just reading them to your kids is good; I still read to my high schoolers up through graduation!) Yet we're so scared that they won't learn or that they won't learn *enough*. I am now convinced that the very same thing will happen –they won't learn *enough*–if we are relying on prepared curriculum for our education! We do use a bit of canned curriculum, but it's not the fabric out of which the majority of our educational program is woven.

Rather than looking to curriculum to give you a false sense of security that education is taking place, I encourage you to look to the Lord for a renewing of your mind. Everyone in America needs it! Ask God what His idea of education is. There is much joy and freedom in His ways–no matter what area of our lives. But His ways must first be sought out and understood. Today's idea of education is very far from God's way, Wisdom's Way–of education.

How do we know whether any given form of education is God's way? Look at the fruit it produces. Look at the current methods of education. They are producing the fruit of burn-out, frustrated people who have a pile of knowledge poured into their heads, but little if any character and values. God's ways produce the fruit of peace, delight, and freedom. And I'm not talking about the flesh-pleasing, selfish, "I-gotta-be-me" kind of freedom the world offers; I'm talking about the freedom Jesus died for us to have in Him! "Where the Spirit of the Lord is, there is liberty."

Unschooling Christianity

by M. Simms

When asked to fill out the religion slot on the hospital form, I would write Christian. There wasn't much else about me to identify me as such though. I believed in God, but He just wasn't relevant to my life.

I was brought up in a very religious household and had more than a passing acquaintance with the Bible. I liked the book and owned one, but I hadn't read it much since I grew up and left home. Nevertheless, I had assimilated certain values, a belief in truth and a creator who had served me well, though unacknowledged.

Time passed. I married and life went on much as before. Then I had a baby, an experience that I found overwhelming and wonderful. I wanted to be a perfect mother and I read every book I could get my hands on. I would breast feed, of course. Off I went to La Leche League meetings to see what I could learn. I found I could trust the information the leaders provided. It satisfied the two basic criteria I needed: scientific validity and consistency with my belief in the rightness of creation. There were some women who homeschooled their children. I was mildly curious, but dismissive of the practice as a little too weird for me to want to try myself.

More time passed and school was in the offing. I enrolled my eldest in Sunday school to learn about God and in Kindergarten to learn the three R's.

The Kindergarten teacher was terrific and things were going well. But, as the year wore on, I noticed something disturbing. My child, who always loved to learn and who had an amazing attention span, was losing both these qualities. Previously, when he had shown an interest in a subject, we had gone off to the library and returned with armloads of books and then repeated the process for weeks and months. Now, if he became interested in something at school, the subject automatically disappeared at the end of the month. Soon his interest did, too. His attention span plummeted.

Concerned, I started reading up on education. I remembered the name John Holt from my earlier brush with homeschoolers, and the local library had a number of books by him. I was impressed by *How Children Learn*. There was much truth and sound observation which resonated with my own experience. Then I read *How Children Fail*. Again, the veracity of his observations were undeniable. So much in the school system was setting up children for failure. I knew I wanted to unschool my children, and after much discussion and delay, I started to do just that. Academically, I felt I had made a sound choice.

But now I was forced to face another truth. If John Holt was right and I really couldn't argue with him since he just made so much sense, then Sunday school wouldn't teach my children much of value about God or the Bible. In fact just the opposite might occur—it may turn them off learning about God. If I really thought these were important subjects to study, then it was necessary that they become an integral part of our home.

I honestly didn't know where to start. My life was entirely secular in nature. I couldn't recreate my childhood, my husband's disinterest in religion found no parallel with my father's obsession with it, and I was only lukewarm myself. I didn't want the "we have the truth and they don't" type of religion I grew up with anyway.

There was the Bible—that book I liked, but didn't read. Maybe I could start by reading it and Bible stories to the kids. I made a New Year's resolution that I would read the Bible—not verse by verse aloud, as my childhood had been full of, but book by book, as I would read any book.

I kept that New Year's resolution better than most. I am still reading the Bible regularly four years later. Abandoning the verse by verse, chapter by chapter method of reading was the best thing I ever did in my search for spiritual truth. I discovered that the many and various doctrines of the many and various Christian denominations are so contradictory and numerous because they just aren't that important in scripture. Looking minutely at each word or verse for absolute truth can blind one to that truth.

What is important comes through loud and clear: loving God, loving one another, forgiving, doing good, protecting the weak and helping the poor, caring for our families and extending that care to others, not placing value on money or high positions or worrying about the future, but focusing on living peacefully and joyfully together.

I learned that I had much to learn. I read words describing fools and they were about me. At times the learning process was very painful, but God had lessons for me in my life and in the Bible. I learned to pray again as I had when I was a child. I prayed for wisdom. I prayed for my family and others, as well as myself. I prayed for the Spirit of God love, light and truth to work in my heart.

I've come a long way. But I slide back so easily, it's scary. Old habits die hard and sometimes my children see no examples of spiritual growth from me for months at a time, and I lose touch with the Bible. Church has become more valuable to me as I recognize the value of associating with others who put the search for God's truth and love in the forefront of their lives. I realize that institutionalized religion can be as destructive to the soul as institutionalized schooling can be to the mind. At times I equate church attendance with religion, and using that as an excuse for not expending the personal effort needed to find my way to God's kingdom. I am still in the process of "deschooling" my own religious experience, so that I can truly love my fellow men and women wholeheartedly, without institutional labels or biases. I have far to go, as bitterness and anger fill my heart too often, pushing out God's love. But now, I have a direction to follow.

I've turned my back on the religion of my parents. They walked their own road to find God and now I must follow my own path to the same goal.

A-Mazing Unit Studies

by Teraisa J. Goldman

The best things in life are not only free, they are rarely planned. Especially good education. And so it was, that beautiful and sunny autumn day my girls and I ventured to Lattin Farms, Fallon, Nevada, to embark on the best unit study we ever stumbled across.

We had read in the morning paper about this particular farm and corn mazes. Immediately, my three girls were donning their sweaters and heading for the door. As we drove, the sky darkened with clouds and sprinkles of rain.

"Do you think it'll be raining at the farm, Mom?"

"Well, it was sunny at our house, only miles back, but you never really know. It could be." The car was quiet for a moment, each of us thinking about the weather spoiling the adventure.

"Did you know I have a friend in Australia right now who is asleep in the dark?"

The topic change threw them off for a moment, but they soon understood, as I continued, "Australia is so far away from where we are, they are not only experiencing night while we have daylight, but they are also a day ahead. What," I asked, "do you think an Australian might be wearing on Christmas Day?"

"I know! They wear clothes like Eskimos, big furry coats and clunky boots," my middle child proudly announced.

"Not exactly."

"Well, they probably dress like us. Aren't most people the same no matter where in the world they live?"

I told my oldest daughter that is probably true in many big countries, but we are concerned with the time and the season.

"In Australia, when we are experiencing Autumn, they are enjoying Spring. What do you think they wear now, during the Christmas season?"

"A bathing suit?" I smiled. They caught on. For the last leg of the trip to Lattin Farms, they talked about different clothes, seasons and countries.

"There it is," one child yelled. The farm signs were now in full view.

Although we were making the trek to walk the corn maze, we would be pleasantly surprised to find so much more to the farm. The owners, Rick and Ann, came and introduced themselves and asked the girls questions such as why they weren't in school today.

"We came to get lost in your corn!" the little one said.

"Before you do," Ann said, "would you like to see our sunflowers? They are as tall as you are!" I watched the walk toward the sunflowers while I talked a moment more with Ann.

When she learned we were unschoolers, she told us to expect to spend the entire day at the farm. She had plenty of hands-on projects for the girls and fresh fruit if they got hungry.

Rick called the kids over and we walked through his collection of antique farm equipment. The girls were allowed to touch and were somewhat interested, but I could tell they wanted to get to the corn maze. Each year, we were told, the maze changes themes. This year's theme was pirates. The cornstalks were about eight feet tall and there was no way to see above them. You are literally like the rat in a scientific rat maze.

"There are two bridges. One is brown. On that bridge, there will be a pirate," said Rick. "Ask for hints, but beware!" We listened to a few more directions before heading into the fields.

Whenever we came to a dead end, there were plaques on wooden tables to read. They told legends of hidden treasures throughout Nevada. More history, this time laced with mythological literature.

Twenty minutes later, we were running into the same dead ends. I was wondering how many acres we were walking without leaving the small spot we were stuck in.

"My legs are tired," my daughter whined, "let's find the brown bridge and ask the pirate how to get out." A little physical education never hurt anyone, but I was tired, too.

"Let the little one lead the way, then." I figured if I couldn't find our way out, it wouldn't hurt to let her be the leader... something she doesn't get to experience very often.

She surprised everyone. Without the pirate, she had led us to the white "exit" bridge in about ten minutes. The bridge is very high and you must cross it to exit the maze. When we got to the top, we were stunned by the breathtaking view. We could see for miles. We laughed as we looked down into the maze, which looked uncomplicated from that position.

Picking raspberries was fun for my kids but soon the air grew cooler. We did not have a watch, but we could tell from the sun's position it was about five o'clock.

"We need to head back, Dad's going to come home soon and miss us." We went back to the entrance and thanked Rick and Ann for having us. They told us there was much more to do, we thanked them again, but said we had to get back home. The skies were clouding and it was beginning to darken.

The day had been fulfilling, fun and educational. History, math, geography, physical education, science, agriculture, fashion, map skills... what more was there to learn?

Well, you simply cannot expect a day like that to escape easily. We talked about it all the way home. It seemed there were more questions on the way home than there were on the way to the farm. I answered what I could and made mental notes to find the answers to the more difficult questions at home.

As I researched encyclopedias and the Internet for the serious answers, the girls drafted thank you notes to the Lattin Farm owners. And it didn't end there. We created malted raspberry shakes and raspberry waffles. We made plans to grow corn next season.

Last night, my youngest daughter regaled us with a well known children's fairy tale: Rapunzal. It seems the fair maiden with the long blonde hair needed, once again, to be rescued from a high tower. The Prince braved his way through the corn maze to get to her. All the other would-be-rescuers got lost in the corn never to be found again.

Chapter Thirteen

Guided by the Lord

To wait on the Lord and allow him to guide our actions is one of the most important parts of Christianity. We followed the Lord's leading when we decided to homeschool our children and we followed him as he guided us closer and closer to the relaxed, unschooling lifestyle of learning we use today. Many parents have had similar experiences as they learn to lean on His strengths instead of their own.

Trusting God is a process of getting to know Him and realizing that He is indeed trustworthy. We can trust Him with our lives, our families and our homeschools. In our walk, we take baby steps toward that trust. I'm not saying that the Lord is going to lead everyone into an unschooling lifestyle, though I do believe if we were trusting in God more we would all be increasingly relaxed in every aspect of our lives. I believe that God will lead you to the place in your homeschool where He will help you with each day, show you the gifts He has given your children and help you to make choices regarding those gifts. It is impossible to do that by buying into someone else's agenda of what school should be like.

Try spending some concentrated time every week focusing on what God wants your children to learn. What gifts is He trying to show you? What character traits does the Lord want honed in your child? What activities this week are in line with His plan? Which are *you* forcing? When I take the time to do this, I too often realize that I've been pushing my own plans, wishes and agendas, rather than the Lord's. The price I pay in stress and futility is high.

The following essays are wonderful examples of families paying close attention to the guidance of the Lord. It's an encouragement to see the

Lord working in the lives of other unschoolers, bringing about the blessings He so wants to bestow on us if we will only follow His leading.

Thoughts on Unschooling the Faith

by Kathy Ward

You shall love the Lord your God with all your heart, with all your soul, and with all your strength. And these words which I command you today shall be in your heart. You shall teach them diligently to your children, and shall talk of them when you sit in your house, when you walk by the way, when you lie down, and when you rise up.~Deuteronomy 6: 5-7

I remember singing a chorus of Deuteronomy 6:5 many years ago in church. I remember looking at the verse in my Bible. It was the year before we began homeschooling and as I looked at the three verses I saw them with new eyes. I saw them with my mother-eyes. Suddenly it wasn't just a dusty passage a few thousand years old given to a people in another part of the world, a people who had given me an enormous spiritual heritage, to be sure. Suddenly I realized that those verses sang to my soul.

As I thought about this passage and read it over I concluded that the unschoolish thrust to it was going to work its way into our style of homeschooling. found that the Hebrew word for "teach diligently" in this passage had the implication of "to pierce" or to "impress into, to imprint, or to engrave." I began pursuing the idea that the kids were going to understand Christianity by means of natural learning, by seeing Christianity as a way of life where faith and God's word are entwined with real life more than by any kinds of compulsory Bible reading or memory verses.

I'm "unschoolish" in all facets of my life. I've always liked to think of Jesus as being kind of an unschooler, walking through fields, talking and discussing. Stopping by the wayside with the disciples, eating and talking some more...I don't think it's a concept foreign to Christianity in any way. Jesus spoke in parables, he taught by object lessons. The countryside and the city were the classroom. Whether he was speaking to a multitude amassed on a hillside above the lake of Galilee, or walking with his disciples through a grain field, healing the sick, comforting those who were outcast, his style of imparting knowledge was a natural one.

A friend of mine, who is Jewish, thinks that unschoolishness is an essential part of Judaism, though it's not identified as "unschooling" of course. The way she explained it to me is that Jews do not use the word "teaching" when referring to the study of Torah. Say a Rabbi is teaching Bereshis (Genesis) to a youngster. He doesn't say "I am teaching Bereshis to this youngster." Instead he will say, "I am learning Bereshis with this youngster." She stressed to me that this is not semantics, it's not contrived, it's a very real, serious and integral part of her culture.

I love the concept of unschooling and it's in no way at variance with the deepest roots of my faith. How many times over the years I've read, heard or been told that "Christians Mustn't Unschool." Although I've held out and not seen eye to eye with that point of view, it has caused me to keep my mouth shut on certain occasions about just what takes place in our home. I've gone into certain situations in years past as an undercover radical unschooler. I'm completely out in the open now and I'm so glad to see a growing crowd of Christian families who want to enjoy learning this way.

Our faith is so interwoven in our lives that matters of the spirit are likely to come up all through the day. We chat, we discuss, sometimes we debate. We pull out the Bible, we look at different translations, we look at various books, some quite controversial. We use commentaries, dictionaries, maps, history books, videos, television programs, movies, music and any other resource we can find that's relevant. Many times we'll pause our discussions and debates to look things up. Did I mention that we argue? Iron sharpening iron, my kids help me define what it is I believe sometimes. My husband and I have returned the favor by being interested in the ways that our kids define what it is that they believe.

Our Christianity does flavor our family interactions but we do not see being parents as being the administrators of a Christian-school-in-the-home as do many we have known over the years. We are fellow travelers with our children. I see us all as disciples together. Sometimes we mentor them (or help them find someone who will) and we always hope to encourage them. Often they encourage us. We pray together, we look into the Bible together, we discuss ideas and some hard issues together, we ask forgiveness when we blow it, we investigate what and why we believe and strive to grow in faith as fellow disciples. My hope is that we give each other the freedom and grace to grow toward God.

Our younger kids enjoy Bible story books. We have quite a collection. I like to collect illustrated story books and examine different styles of art—from cartoons to classical. I've begun collecting small reproductions of religious art, from the medieval Madonnas to Van Gogh, and beyond. I have a beautiful, huge family Bible with Rembrandt's paintings and drawings of Old and New Testament scenes that is awesome.

One step outside our door and we are in the vast Mojave Desert, a fascinating portion of Creation for sure. We have spent many hours observing the wildlife. Our children have a respect and love for the natural world because they have been fortunate enough to be able to spend many hours living in it. We've studied native plants. We've observed and collected the rocks that wash down the hillsides from the San Gabriel Mountains. We've watched the birds, small animals and reptiles. We've seen coyotes loping across our yard in the evening. We've watched in awe as a Bald Eagle has swooped low across our chicken pen and flown off. The weather here includes winds, rolling thunderstorms, hail, flash floods, lightening, summertime electrical storms, winter snows, heat and twisters.

When we've gone outside and taken the time to look and contemplate what is around us we've been able understand to the core what Romans 1:20 means, "For since the creation of the world His invisible attributes are clearly seen, being understood by the things that are made, even His eternal power and divine nature..." Nature is a potent teacher about God and being connected with the natural world has given us many opportunities to talk about and reflect upon who God is. The desert sky at night has provided more food for thought among our children, as we gaze and remember that the heavens do, in fact, declare the glory of God.

Music is another way to touch the spiritual in our kids. We share the spiritual music we love with our children. Some they like and some doesn't do anything for them. With eight children, though, chances are good someone's going to be touched. My husband is a musician and this makes it fun, but barely musical me can still put on a beautiful tape or a CD.

Here's something that's specific to our family that may not apply to everyone. We are wanting to incorporate more of the liturgical year into our family life. We have been so very blessed by celebrating Advent for many years and last year I didn't want the celebration to end. The softly flickering candles, the scent of the beeswax, the pine boughs, the beautiful, awesome story of the Nativity, children listening, baby fidgeting and teenager reading. Then there was the special Christmas music, the quiet prayers and going outside to look at the stars and imagine...feeling the Presence. I'm not persuaded that we have to wait for Christmas time every year to have this. I'm busy and distracted so much of the time and celebrating the Nativity this way helps me to slow down and focus. The Ancient Church set aside times to do this and it was good. I want it. I think this kind of celebration can help the children get a hold of what it's all about. I think that the early church knew what it was doing when it celebrated various Holy days throughout the year. I think that this kind of celebration can feed the soul.

Having been in American evangelical circles for many years where this is at best ignored and at worst treated as "empty ritual" I feel like a starving person with a whole banquet spread before me. It's been there all along, but I haven't paid attention to it for over 15 years. There is a whole year of beauty and history and celebration and significant ritual spread out before me and my family. We're going to partake!

My husband was raised in a liturgical church and I spent time in and out of one in early adulthood. There were beauty and riches there that we feel like we left behind. In fact for the last year we've been attending a liturgical church (ELCA) as a family. So we are on a search for a way to bring the Church Calendar into our home in a way that speaks to our family.

As years have passed and as we've grown as parents and become Grandparents, we've found that the One we trust can truly be trusted with our children and with their lives, hearts, desires, hopes, dreams and faith. In the early years we were apt to do Bible memory drills and participate actively in various children's Bible clubs (thus proving a friend's theory that nearly every unschooler struggles with a desire to school something from time to time). As time has gone by we've seen that feeding the spiritual hunger that is in our kids' hearts can be done in less stringent, less structured ways and be just as effective. Some children do really want to pursue a serious study of the Bible and some do so in a structured way. Other children delve into it in a more freeform manner.

One of our daughters has taken the first two books of the Old Testament and drawn cartoons (similar to those in the Beginner's Bible) to illustrate each of the chapters. They are insightful and interesting cartoons and she uses them to tell the stories to her younger siblings. The same daughter is now reading through various books of the Bible as her interest leads. Two sons have a pointed interest in Bible prophecy. One child takes copious notes from her study sources, another doesn't particularly want to take notes but chooses to discuss things as they cross his mind and grab his attention. One son specializes in arguing, er, debating difficult issues.

In the early years of parenting we were given dire warnings about what would happen to our kids if we didn't do X, Y and Z with regard to their spiritual education. We made sure that we did plenty of X, Y and Z. From the vantage point of having withdrawn from a very legalistic, very demanding practice of Christianity, I can say that I feel quite sure that the younger kids have a faith as strong as and every bit as vibrant as the kids who were X-ed, Y-ed and Z-ed. The younger kids are definitely more able to express their doubts, reservations and perhaps their outlandish-sounding theories than were their older siblings.

As seasoned parents, we're more unflappable, less apt to worry about them taking off on rabbit trails. And I'm far less apt to worry when their path diverges from the one I'm on. It's important for me to work on understanding where their pursuit of God takes them. Sometimes it seems like we're walking together, other times we seem to be separated by the trees as their path branches off of the one I'm on. I always want to work on remaining within shouting distance of my children, this is part of the work I do as a mother. Truly their relationship to and with God is their own, not mine, and they deserve and need the time, space and freedom to sort things out and to delve into what they truly believe. My husband and I have placed these children we love into the hands of the One we trust, the One who loves all of Creation, the One who has pulled us from the fire more than once. We do all that we can, we walk by our kids, and we trust in His grace and love to pull our kids through the fires and the trials of their lives. So far it's working.

Reprinted by permission from Gentle Spirit Magazine, June 1999

Fending off the Fears

by Colleen Jeffrey

I woke up at 4:08 the other morning to the sound of the cat scratching on my daughter's bedroom door. I lay awake, bleary-headed, listening to her scrape away, hoping she'd manage to pry the door open herself and get in. No such luck. After she'd resurfaced the door for minutes on end, there was silence, then a plaintive mew. I sighed and got up. Apparently I am the only person in the house who can hear this sort of thing. I opened the door for the kitty, who gave me a "Well, it's about time!" look before sauntering in. I heard her crunching her cat food as I clumped down the stairs to the bathroom.

Back in bed, I stared at the ceiling—actually, being very nearsighted, I stared into the overhead blur—and realized I wouldn't be asleep again any time soon. My husband was still sleeping soundly, so quiet conversation was out. What can you do, awake in the wee hours but too groggy to read? On a good night, in a peaceful mood, I pray. On an average night, I worry.

After I've cataloged all the possible exits from the house in case there were a fire, and decided what I'd grab first to throw out the window (old letters, journals, the dogs) and carry out with me (kids, guitars), and then after I've calculated how much dental work I'll probably need and wondered how we'll pay for it, I usually get around to stewing in my anxieties about the children's educational futures.

This particular night, in that four a.m. spookhouse hush, Fear came and sat on my chest like an obese housecat. Breathing became tricky. This fear had something to say and I was stuck there, flat on my back, listening.

"Are your kids going to be okay?" it breathed. (Fear has cold, acidic, tinny breath, like a forgotten can of pineapple juice corroding in the fridge.) "Are you doing right by them?"

"Not now, please," I groaned, under my breath. The Fear pursed its lips. I recalled my third grade teacher Mrs. Prisbane, wagging a gnarled finger at me.

"What if they never learn the things they're supposed to? What then?"

We've been through this, I thought feebly. *Unschooling seems to be the best way for my family to go. I've considered all these questions before, and just because right now I'm too tired to remember the answers, doesn't mean there aren't any.*

The Fear waited with condescending patience for me to finish, then pounced. "But what about all the facts they're missing?" it said ominously. "The gaps."

I squirmed. The Fear shifted tactics, adopted an earnest tone of concern. "Of course you want the best for your children," it rasped. "You don't want them to lack valuable skills and knowledge, to feel inferior and ashamed. So the best thing you can do for them," the Fear leaned in, its eyes gleamed red, and the smile grew taut around its teeth, "is to MAKE them learn!"

I sweated with shame and frustration. It must be true—I wasn't pushing my kids hard enough to succeed. They were bound to end up poor, unhappy, ignorant, unemployable bums, a disgrace to the family, loping around using drugs and double negatives. "Help," I prayed.

A slim flash of wisdom came. Should I really be trying to solve this tonight?

No, most definitely not. I felt a wry smile loosen the grim tension around my mouth. "Dear God, I give this tangle to you." I sighed, rolled over, and flattened the Fear with my pillow. "I'll think about this tomorrow," I decided, like Scarlett O'Hara.

But the Fear had a parting shot. "So you're prepared to let your children fail!" it sniped, faintly.

"I'm not listening," I mumbled into the pillow.

The next day I was groggy and discouraged. I've been a pretty easy mark for Fear lately; two of our four kids are now young teenagers. They were sweet, shy homebodies to start with. Now they spend even more time cocooned indoors, insulated to go through all the big hormonal changes on the way to adulthood. While the younger two children stump me with questions about life, or dance off to friends' houses or ballet practice, the teens lock into computer games or linger in their rooms, figuring things out.

It's a time of inward focus for them, a needful time, but without much visible "progress" for a fretful mom to monitor. I know they're good kids, but will they really turn out okay? Am I doing enough of the right things for them and with them? During any given day, my level of confidence can bound from high to low and back again, over and over, like a gymnastic terrier. I keep finding my shoulders hunched up around my ears. Each time this happens, I have to exhale loudly and lever them down again.

But the nighttime battles are the hardest. In the grip of my late-night worries, I forget all that my children are doing and learning, when the Fear reminds me in a hiss of all that they are NOT doing or learning yet. Suddenly it seems like a good idea to go wake them right now, sit them up in bed, and have a little chat about, oh, say, the principal exports of Cameroon, or how many board feet of lumber Mr. Smith needs to complete his duodecahedral barn.

Then in the daylight, I remember I've been trying to trust God to guide us all through this unschooling adventure, and I feel foolish for having let my fears bully me again. How will I ever know the peace our Lord promised while anxiety holds ground in my mind? And I'm no good to the kids if I seize up.

This Fear had assaulted me one time too many. I was determined to pin it down, study it and answer it the best I could. So that afternoon, when I sensed my Fear dozing, I jostled it awake. It blinked and huddled, looking much wispier than I remembered and with fewer teeth.

"Hi!" I said. "You know that conversation we were having last night? Well, I have a couple of things to add. Hold still." Fears don't often hold up well under close examination. This one squirmed to get back in the shadows, but I held it firmly.

"Listen, I think the reason you can get the best of me is that I've made some faulty assumptions about my kids and learning and God's care." I pulled out a notebook and reflected a minute before starting a list. The Fear frowned and squinted at it.

<u>Assumptions I Realize I Have Been Making:</u>

1. The world is not interesting enough to grab my children's attention and motivate them to learn.
2. Despite all my fervent prayers to the contrary, God might allow my children to slide through life never knowing or being stirred up to learn important truths.

3. If they appear at any moment to be failing or lagging in the task of becoming whole, alive, informed and conscientious people, it's somehow my fault.

When I leaned back to reread the list, I was agape and giggling. "Do you see how ridiculous you are?" I teased the Fear, but it had slunk out of sight at some point. I reflected again. "Or maybe it's me who's ridiculous, taking these ideas seriously for so long, never examining them like this. I can see I'm still trying to take responsibility for absolutely everything my kids learn or do, which is impossible, of course, not to mention overwhelming and unnecessary. Gosh, no wonder I get stuck between panic and paralysis."

"So now I suppose you've got everything figured out?" muttered the Fear, sullen and sarcastic.

"No, I don't," I said. "But even when I have to deal with valid concerns, I refuse to be driven by anxiety, or by impatience, or a false sense of shame. There's a verse that says, 'In nothing be anxious…"

"…Except where your offspring are concerned,'" finished the Fear.

"No, no; wrong translation. Oh, it's impossible to reason with you—go back to sleep."

Since that afternoon, the Fear hasn't exactly stopped trying to trip me up. It still weaves between my legs just when I'm starting to hit my stride, and growls surly comments about my multiple limitations and all my children's shortcomings. But there's a difference between Fear's promptings and God's. When God leads, there's a lightness, a sense of moving into freedom and peace, even if the way there is difficult or full of changes. It's a breath of pure air. In contrast, any fear-induced push for "righteousness" feels heavy, condemning, close, squeezing me, leaving no choices.

I have found a use for this Fear and, surprisingly, I'm even learning to be grateful for its attacks. By decimating my own self-confidence, Fear can point me towards God's grace and sufficiency. "Oh, yeah!," I remember, "I'm not running this show." This view reminds me of what I can do:

I can remain committed to following God's will as it's revealed, step by step, duty by duty, and trust Him to do the rest.

I can commit my children's lives to God, asking Him to supply them with a thirst for learning and the ability to satisfy that thirst.

I can let them know I look to Him for guidance and wisdom, and I can pray with them, asking Him to lead us in our learning each day and give us grace to see how it all declares His glory.

I can admit my limitations to my children. I'll be as honest with them about my own desires, hopes and failures as I can be—and be open to theirs in turn.

God leads me into the lessons from life that I need—can't I expect Him to do this for my kids as well? I pray and work and wait in hope. I take comfort from something George MacDonald wrote: "The only way to get at what is right is to do what seems right. Even if we make a mistake there is no other way!"

There are other practical steps I'm learning, too; specific actions I can take when I can't seem to shake my worries. There's better company to keep than Fear, so I go and sit with my children. I relax in their smiles and their banter. I ask them how they're doing. Settling into the moment, seeing the people they are now, reassures me about who they'll become.

Then again, some moments are crazy-making. Quarrels, whining, nagging. Talking with my husband helps calm a lot of frustrations. He graciously listens to me vent, but I don't want to overburden him. Sometimes a good brisk walk works best, gets me out of the house and helps me retrieve some perspective. Later at home I might dive into old journal entries or photo albums to remember the good times and take heart; remember the bad times and see how far my kids have come. We've pulled out of slumps before—this too shall pass.

And when Fear leaps on me at four a.m., breathing corrosive questions, I just won't listen. I'll stick my fingers in my ears if I have to; hum some little chorus of courage under my breath, at least until my husband rolls over and pulls his pillow on top of his head. Then I'll tell the Fear, "Hey—go bother the cat."

Our Unschooling Family

by Kathie Smith

I don't know if we fit everyone's definitions of an unschooling family, but over the past three years we have changed and evolved from the typical school family into one that learns at every opportunity. When we moved from our home in May of 1997 our children were enrolled in a private Christian school. At that time we had a son in the fourth grade, another in second grade and a daughter in Kindergarten. I knew that we would not be able to continue the private school education in our new town, and our family did not see the public education as an option. Without those two options, I was forced to consider homeschooling. I remember wondering if there were any "normal people" who educated their children at home. Then I began to read about home education and the Lord began to speak to my heart.

I was working as a full time Kindergarten aide at the time, and I was always so tired and worn out. I didn't have much left to give of myself at the end of the day. Along with my job, my husband and I have served as youth pastors for the past ten years. I was always in a battle to catch up... never having enough time. Family life was hard to fit in. As I began to read about homeschooling, God continued to soften my heart to the idea of bringing my children home. I can recall praying and asking the Lord if this is what He wanted us to do. My husband and I began to feel confident that God was leading us in this direction and assuring us that He would show us how to do it.

As the time came nearer and nearer to move, I came across this verse: "All your children shall be taught by the Lord, and great shall be the peace of your children." Isaiah 54:13. From that day on I knew that I could rely on Him, I didn't have to worry because He was in control of my children's education. Still, on those days when I am unsure, I look upon those words and feel confident in God's plan for my children.

I wish that I could tell you that was the end of all my worry, but it wasn't! I spent the next couple of years trying to do "school at home". It involved two years of feeling guilty because I could never accomplish all of my lesson plans. There was a whole list of things that I couldn't do and I was beginning to get a bit frustrated and discouraged. The funny thing about being a mom, it seems when you are frustrated and discouraged it spreads to the whole family! We were all really getting uptight. Teaching always seemed forced and not natural.

On my behalf, I do have to say there were some great moments. My dear sweet daughter did learn how to read and we became a lot closer to one another and to the Lord. However, the words of that verse were always in my mind... *The Lord shall teach my ... And great shall be their peace.* Okay, where was this peace? I wasn't finding much of that. I did find a retreat in the Internet. After we got a new computer we went online and I was surely amazed! I found a whole community of homeschooling families. I found myself constantly finding those little moments of "peace" where I could sneak away and thentwo really great things happened .

First of all I learned that there were people that didn't use a curriculum! I couldn't believe that. I thought they were crazy—no rules, no limitations? I listened to some very patient unschoolers as they shared their thoughts and ideas with me. The thought that learning could happen all the time, with no prior preparation or scheduling? Impossible!

As I thought about these things, God began to speak to my heart again. I began to look at my children, to watch them as they played together. One morning it all sunk in. I had assigned my children an oral report on a planet. My oldest had prepared a great report however, he did not present it very well. With tears coming down his face he communicated his sense of failure. We sat down together and I held him in my arms and I felt like the failure. I was not teaching my son important things he needed, I was teaching him how to hate learning. I was teaching him how to fear expressing himself and all the God given abilities that he had been blessed with.

That day I decided enough was enough. I was going to trust that God would teach them. I had to let go of the idea that I was solely in charge of making them into the great people that God wanted them to be. I needed to be confident that God had put into each one of my children the natural gifts and abilities that they needed. What I needed to do was to be an example for them, to love the Lord my God, and to be able to communicate that in a way that would be desirable to them. I needed to be their model to emulate. This is still not an easy thing. I always want to step in and try to direct their path myself, but God is faithful, He continues to remind me and to show me that He is the one who is always in control.

One of the best things that has happened since we started to "unschool" is the freedom. The freedom to be who God has made us to be. I like that my 11-year-old isn't limited to the constraints of peer pressure. Recently he informed me that he wanted to teach at one of our weekly Jr. High youth group meetings. He prepared the whole evening himself. The night he was to teach we ended up combining our Jr. and Sr. High so that there was a bigger and older group than usual. This change didn't affect his determination to share the message that God had put on his heart. God provided an opportunity for an oral presentation that my son will never forget. There was no grade given, no stickers or ribbons, but a sense of confidence and accomplishment that is now part of who he is today. Learning doesn't have to be scheduled to be productive or valuable. We don't have to manipulate our kids to learn all that we think is important. We do have to listen to the Lord and take His direction for our children. We need to help them to hear the voice of the Lord themselves, to be obedient to the calling upon their lives, to realize that they can serve God now. That is the best education we can provide .

The other thing that I learned during my first couple of months online is that I need to spend time daily with the Lord in order to be a model for my children. I need to be able to hear His voice so I can help my children strive for His wisdom. I was soon convicted that I wasn't nearly as excited about spending those precious minutes with the Lord as I was in finding those minutes to be online. So, God can even speak to us through our shortcomings. I am still learning daily even though I am not tested at the end of the week. I have learned many things since I graduated from formal schooling, but I know that I learn best when it is me that is pressing ahead to figure something out or learn something new. That is what I want for my children—to love learning and always have their eyes open to what the Lord wants to show them. I do not want them restrained with trying to find the right answer to someone else's problem, but to know how to find God's answer for theirs.

Lastly, I can say I believe that my children finally have a peace that only comes when you close out the plans and ideas set by the someone else and listen to what God's plans for you are. They have a childhood I wished that I had, with the freedom to explore, to notice and ask questions, to sing and rejoice aloud as we work and to take the time to notice those little lessons that come so easily from the Lord as we walk about our day. Unschooling, or by my own definition; child led learning, developing the natural God given inclinations, talents and gifts, has freed me from the pressure of making sure I don't fail my children academically, to trusting solely on the Lord's faithfulness to my children.

Proverbs 3: 5,6 states: "Trust in The Lord with all your heart and lean not on your own understanding; In all your ways acknowledge him and He will make your paths straight." Trust in the Lord, listen for his guidance, don't rely on your own understanding or that of the world. Model that to your children, and then walk the path that God sets before you, and don't be surprised if that path is letting your children step out of the school box and walk the path that God laid for them.

Many Celebrations

by Shannon Timura

There is much written on how to follow a packaged Christian program, but not much on how to simply follow and trust the Lord, His inspired Word and our own natural talents. My husband and I have been blessed with three energetic children. Samuel is seven, Abigail is five and Joseph is one. Unschooling is perfectly delicious. We have the freedom to do real activities and teach life skills rather than subjects. For example, we teach alphaphonics approximately twenty minutes a day for six months when the children are ready to read. This has shown tremendous benefits. Once this extremely simple, no props book is completed, the library becomes an adventure, guided by Mom of course.

Following an artificial Bible, math, reading science, physical education, music, art or history workbook centered program would bog our family down. There wouldn't be time to do the more time consuming projects such as gardens, lemonade stands, animal care, volunteering, cookie baking and packaging for others, snow forts and make believe. Our family also launched a creative program called Cousin Chronicles this year. It is a monthly publication highlighting the talents and activities of my children's 14 cousins.

My son, Sam, is the editor. He is learning along with his sister to write articles, draw illustrations, design word puzzles, learn layout skills and the reality of deadlines. (Not to mention the credibility we have gained from relatives regarding schooling at home.)

I strongly believe we've been called by God to educate our children not to shelter but protect and obey the biblical mandate in Deuteronomy 6: 4-9, *"Hear, O Israel! the lord Our God, the Lord is one! And you shall love the Lord your God with all your heart and with all your soul and with all your might. And these words, which I am commanding you today, shall be on your heart, and you shall teach them diligently to your sons and shall talk of them when you sit in your house and when you walk by the way and when you lie down and when you rise up. And you shall bind them as a sign on your hand and they shall be as frontlets on your forehead. And you shall write them on the doorpost of your house and on your gates."*

We are diligent in our Bible studies and have effortlessly gained much knowledge by practicing the Jewish holidays. They open the door for so much fun! The children truly enjoy the planning involved in celebrating Rosh Hashanah, Yom Kipper, Hanukkah, Purim, Tu B' Shevat, Sukkot and even the newer custom of celebrating the birth of the Jewish state of Israel. Yom Hashoa honors victims of the Holocaust and opens up many discussions, relevant and not so relevant, yet very necessary in the development of young minds.

Having a special time each week that we dress up, put out the nice dishes and use our best manners is something our daughter won't let us give up. So the weekly Sabbath, Shabbot, has been formally adopted. Shabbot, a sweet taste of the heaven, traditionally begins each Friday at twilight, and ends after sunset on Saturday night. We have had to adopt this to observe Sunday as our special Sabbath and it begins at Saturday's twilight. Since there is no work to be done during this time, according to the fourth commandment, we have arranged our week around custom. All the household chores are done by 5:00 PM Saturday, including shopping, laundry, ironing and yard care. We dress for the lighting of the candles, dinner and prayers. This gives us all a beautiful sense of completion to our week and something to look forward to at its close.

Many celebrations also make the way for good family relationships. There are crafts to be made, homemade gifts to be given, special recipes and songs to be learned, even plays to be performed and a delightful building, a sukka, to be built during Sukkot. The Bible comes alive when we learn it through shared experiences such as these. Not to mention the advances made in reading, history, and life skills such as manners and hospitality.

The fifteen Jewish observances plus all the Christian and American holidays, birthdays and anniversaries provide a lovely framework for a joyous life. Simply add the people we love, a little creativity and enjoy.

Time Spent With God

by Shannon Schermerhorn

Friday nights are my time to plan the coming week. I sit in the backyard during the cool of the evening, while the wind blows through my half-weed, half-vegetable garden. I spread out a blanket directly in front of the crisp, drying diapers on the line. There is something so serene and spiritual sitting amidst God's creation. I start off my time with prayer, asking the Lord to show me my children's individual gifts and talents. I pray for wisdom to raise them into His specific plan for their life. As I begin noting down what I think we need to work on for each child during the week to come, the Lord always reveals to me little tidbits and insights about their needs and passions. With these things in mind, I then begin to plan the week. What the Lord shows and reveals to me also determines our "library booklist."

Every third Tuesday we go to the library and withdraw about 30 books, audio and videotapes. So off we go to the library, one Mom, four children and three large cloth sacks. We have the most helpful librarian who will bend over backward to help us. She allows me to bring home books listed as 'reference only' and frequently comments, "I thought of you when I came across this book." It is to your family's advantage to get to know your librarian and other employees (and don't forget the cookies once in a while!)

After I have picked out all the essential books needed for whatever we are studying, I go back to the children and help them pick out whatever they are interested in. After about two hours, we are just about through with our library trip. Upon arriving home I usually make cookies as the children all sit in the living room quietly absorbing their books. When the cookies are about done they clean up, get into their night clothes and crawl into our family bed. By now it is dark, and if we are fortunate, the wind is blowing. We love to snuggle up together under blankets while we open all the bedroom windows and the cold air fills the room. I serve hot chocolate chip cookies and cold milk. There in bed, I read their 'picks' by candlelight until we can stay awake no longer.

Are you thinking about unschooling and haven't had the courage to start? Check out some books at the library, go home and make cookies, open the windows in the bedroom, crawl into bed with your children and all their 'picks' and daily ask the Lord to show you what your children need. I can't recommend a better way to begin!

Chapter Fourteen

What about Support Groups?

Some people swear by support groups, while others can do without them altogether. In this chapter we outline some ways that homeschool support groups can be helpful and explain how to start your own.

Oftentimes, if we know there are others like us, we will not feel so alone or unique. Add unschooling into the equation of feeling alone and different, and at some places we feel like we have three heads. No matter what our so-called differences, once we hang with others like us, we begin to hear their stories and their similarities. In doing so we gain confidence and feel accepted. This is one of the reasons I think support groups are important, especially for those just beginning on their journey.

Another huge bonus of homeschool support groups is the opportunity our children have to meet new friends and join group activities. Many groups lean towards family activities and participation is usually free, or request only a nominal fee.

Support groups come in all shapes and sizes. The larger ones can be a little daunting at first, but you can usually come up with good information and, if you're inclined toward political involvement, they are the best place to be. Smaller groups are far more intimate and your children can develop long-lasting friendships there.

Starting an Unschooling Support Group

Well, someone's got to do it! There are a few basic things which have to be decided upon first.

- Will the group be secular or will it have some religious affiliation?

- Will the group have a definite leader or will decisions be made by consensus?
- Where will the meetings be held? Libraries, churches and community centers may offer free space.
- When and how often does your group want to meet?
- Will this be an open group or do you just want a few families involved?

If you don't mind an open, growing group, you might want to publicize your meetings! Run an ad in homeschool newsletters, start a website and give your state group the contact information for your new local group.

Your First Meeting

Here are a few tips to make your first meeting as easy and painless as possible.

- Introduce yourself, talk about expectations and needs.
- Open the floor and listen to others needs and expectations. Take note of what others are looking for.
- Bring up the subject of baby-sitting ... many times adult homeschool meetings are attended by both parents. To encourage this, find a teen, or other suitable person to care for the little ones. Sometimes a nominal fee is charged for this service.
- Provide refreshments if you can. It's a known fact that you get to know people best while eating!
- Be sure to clearly set and announce the date of the next meeting.

Each meeting should have a time for business, a time for sharing and a topic. Guest speakers are a great addition, maybe a Mom or Dad with a particular talent or career will volunteer.

Okay, that wasn't too bad was it? Again, be sure to specify the next meeting date! Ask members for their names/addresses/phone numbers and email addresses, with the assurance they will be kept in confidence. Think about writing up some base policies for your group, the purpose, meeting times, contact name and info. This will be very important to give new members.

Activities

A main element of homeschool support groups is usually the involvement in activities for our families. Here are some tips to keep in mind when booking a trip or activity.

Have all the information available for interested parties. Call the place of interest and make sure they *understand* homeschooling. Explain that there will be many parents and a mixed age group of children. See if there are any age restrictions. Inquire about cost, group rates, eating options, gift shops, stroller accessibility, appropriate clothing, directions, educational tours, where to park...is that all? I'm sure you can think of a few more things to add!

Sometimes support is important in the life of an unschooler while at other times it is less so. I think it depends on where you are at in your unschooling life. When I first began homeschooling, I wanted reassurance. Now that my children are older and we are living a full unschooling lifestyle, I find I don't need as much support. I have been thinking though, that perhaps I should begin to give back by being supportive to others in my area. Support groups are a giving, cyclical thing that returns as much as you give.

If you have trouble finding a group right for you... try following the advice in this chapter and start your own!

Existing Groups

To locate an existing group, try the following comprehensive Internet resources for contact information:

www.nhen.org
The National Home Education Network is an inclusive organization made of homeschoolers, aimed at helping other homeschoolers. The site offers

loads of information, message boards and a searchable database of local and online support groups.

www.home-ed-magazine.com
Home Education Magazine is not only a homeschooling magazine, but a site that has an online newsletter, message boards, articles and much more. Found under "networking," HEM's support group listings are substantial.

Chapter Fifteen

Homeschooling on the Web

There is so much great information on the web that Elissa and I have had to be very selective in our choices. We also took into consideration that websites often come and go in the blink of an eye, so we tried to pick those that seem to have staying power. Some are not strictly unschooling sites, but were chosen for the overall quality of their offerings and helpfulness.

Home Education Magazine
www.home-ed-magazine.com
The site to start with if you are looking for general information. This has active message boards, news and updates, questions and answers, resources and networking. Also includes are current and back issue articles from over 17 years of Home Education Magazine.

Unschooling.com
www.unschooling.com
This site has frequently asked questions on unschooling, an active support email list and wonderful articles. This is the unschooling site to check out. The boards are an education by themselves, filled with thought provoking questions and informative answers.

Growing Without Schooling
www.holtgws.com
This is the site of the Holt Associates and Growing Without Schooling magazine. They have an online bookstore with some of the best unschooling books available. They have a page of quality unschooling links and information on their yearly conference.

Learn In Freedom

www.learninfreedom.org

This is an extensive site that would take ages to navigate if you could indeed see it all. The links and information are almost endless. There are a lot of wonderful articles and essays available.

Family Unschoolers network

www.unschooling.org

The Family Unschoolers Network provides support for unschoolers, homeschoolers and self-directed learners. If you are interested in unschooling, homeschooling, self-directed learning or just learning in general, then this is the site for you! You will find newsletter articles, reviews, resources, web sites, books and lots of other information to help your homeschooling or unschooling efforts.

Jon's homeschooling page

www.midnightbeach.com/hs

This is truly one of the most helpful sites we've uncovered. With over two hundred homeschooling pages you're sure to find what you need. This was one of the first sites I found in my online homeschool information quest several years ago.

A to Z Home's Cool Homeschooling Website

www.gomilpitas.com/homeschooling

A friendly and supportive homeschool community with chat, message boards and deep linking into the best essays about homeschooling to get you started or give you daily inspiration and ideas. Use it to find support groups and laws as you start out. Use it to shop and compare homeschool products and prices. There's even links to lots of free stuff. Decidedly eclectic, there's resources on A to Z for those who unschool, who create their own unit studies, who wish to purchase curriculum, who want the support of distance learning programs or umbrella schools.

Christian Unschooling

www.inspirit.com.au/unschooling

Not to be too prejudiced, but we love our site! It offers state support group info, links on special needs, unschooling, homeschooling, educational links, parenting links, articles, book reviews, a Christian Unschooling E-Zine, message boards and much more. We feel it is a great asset to homeschoolers everywhere.

Eclectic Homeschool Online

www.eho.org

This site has everything! State info, great articles and something for every kind of homeschooler.

Cafi Cohen's Homeschool Teens and College

www.homeschoolteenscollege.net

This site is directed at the homeschooling of 11-18 yr olds! Offers articles, college admission policies, college applications written by homeschoolers and info on Cafi herself. Cafi is the author of *And What About College,* a book that shows how to turn unschooling education into an impressive transcript.

Natural Learning

www.geocities.com/Heartland/Trail/3405/Naturallearning.html

This is a great site to go to meet other internet unschoolers! A mailing list, forum, chat, great articles and a book list are just a few of their many offerings.

The Wright Way to Homeschool

www.geocities.com/wrightway2/index.html

While this is not a completely "established" website, it offers one unschooling family's journal of learning. Follow their learning through 365 days.

The Porch Swing

www.tumon.com/porchswing

The unofficial home of CCU-List on the Internet. Here you can learn what CCU-List is (Christ-Centered Unschooling), and why they affectionately refer to themselves as, "The Porch Swing." The articles were compiled and edited from threads, posted at various times by various members. They include titles such as: What is Deschooling, What is Unschooling, Teaching Children to Read, and Christian vs. Secular Unschooling and many more.

Barb Shelton's Main Page

www.homeschooloasis.com

A totally awesome site which houses a lot of Barb's great articles on homeschooling. Take a look around and be blessed!

Homeschooling Your Child with Special Needs:

http://209.1.224.12/Athens/8259/special.html

Includes e-mail loops, message boards, newsgroups, national & local organizations, other resources and many other resources that offer information and help.

Chapter Sixteen

Resources

About the books chosen here:

We have put together a list of books designed to help the Christian unschooler throughout their journey. Some are authored by Christians, some aren't. Why are we including books that are not obviously Christian? Simple put, there are very few books available on Christian unschooling. We also believe that a book does not have to be written from a Christian world view to contain valuable content. Like all books, Christian or not, you have to hold the contents up to your beliefs and ask, "does this fit?" I have read some books by obvious non Christians and have thought... *that is so right*, and I have read some books by Christians and thought... *what Bible did they get that from?*

We believe the books we chose will be of help unschoolers—either by encouragement or resources. Take the good and leave the rest.

Books

And the Skylark Sings With Me by Albert, David H.

Published by: New Society Publishing, 1999, ISBN 0865714010

Acting on their conviction that to educate a child well is to enable her to find her destiny, David Albert and his partner Ellen listened carefully, with respect and with love, to how their children expressed their own learning needs. Leaving traditional homeschooling methods behind, they followed their daughters' unique knowledge quests from astronomy to botany, opera to mythology and then went about finding the resources and opportunities to meet those needs within their community. Written as a series of friendly and accessible vignettes, *And the Skylark Sings with Me* will reassure parents who are considering homeschooling for the first time, and provides dozens of ideas that families can use in their own learning journeys.

Awakening Your Child's Natural Genius; Enhancing Curiosity, Creativity and Learning Ability by Armstrong, Thomas; Ph.D
Published by: J P Tarcher, 1991, ISBN 0874776082
The premise of this book is that children are natural geniuses. Dr. Armstrong talks about their inborn curiosities and how we, as parents, can help cultivate interests. While this is not a book about homeschooling, Dr. Armstrong writes vividly about how to learn in more natural ways.

In Their Own Way by Armstrong, Thomas Ph.D.
Published by: J P Tarcher, 2000, ISBN 0874774667
This book talks about why schools are not the best choice for many styles of learning and how we as parents can understand what kind of "intelligence" our child possesses, and therefore enable them to learn in a way that benefits them best. Very important book for parents to read, as it gives concrete examples of different learning styles and examples of how to teach for each different one.

And What about College? How Homeschooling Can Lead to Admissions to the Best Colleges & Universities by Cohen, Cafi
Published by: Holt Associates, 2000, ISBN 0913677116
This is an informative book for anyone with older children. In a very clear cut and easy to read manner Cafi Cohen takes the mystery out of applying for college and the records needed to do so.

Homeschooling: The Teen Years (Your Complete Guide to Successfully Homeschooling the 13- to 18-Year-Old) By Cohen, Cafi
Published by: Prima Publishing, 2000, ISBN: 0761520937
With today's growing parental concern about the safety, negative social pressures and questionable teaching effectiveness in our nation's high schools, many parents are opting to teach their teenagers at home. With

real-life stories from dozens of families who have traveled the homeschooling road successfully, this book reveals the adventure and rewards as well as the special challenges of working with this age group.

Homeschooling for Excellence by Colfax, David & Micki
Published by: Warner Books, 1998, ISBN 0446389862
A classic book by a pioneering homeschooling family. It is a descriptive story of two parents who learn to trust their children's educational choices. Includes wonderful resource chapters.

The Gift of Dyslexia: Why Some of the Smartest People Can't Read and How They Learn by Davis, Ronald, D.
Published by: Perigee, 1997, ISBN 039952293X
This book is a MUST for any parent whose child seems to be struggling with a learning disability. The author himself has dyslexia, but at a late age discovered that he has many great gifts. This book talks about what dyslexia is, what it isn't, and the gifts that accompany it. The second half of this book is a step-by-step practical approach to helping, mostly by using symbol mastery.

The Homeschooling Book of Answers by Dobson, Linda
Published by: Prima Publishing, 1998, ISBN 0761513779
This is a wonderfully thick book, when you heft it, you are reassured that the 88 most respected voices in homeschooling really are going to answer your questions. You won't be disappointed. Written in question and answer format the book is easy to read and extremely informative.

Homeschooling the Early Years; Your Complete Guide to Successfully Homeschooling the 3- to 8- Year-Old Child by Dobson, Linda
Published by: Prima Publishing, 1999, ISBN 0761520287
The formative years are the most critical to a child's education. They lay the foundation for developing learning skills that last a lifetime. For that

reason, homeschooling during those early years takes on considerable importance to parents dissatisfied with traditional schools.

The Art of Education: Reclaiming Your Family, Community and Self by Home Education by Dobson, Linda
Published by: Holt Associates, 1997, ISBN 0913677140
This book is a must read for anyone who feels the longing for something more for your family. Education is an art that all of us can and should practice. This is a rare book, one that will stay with you long after you read it, giving you the empowerment to change your family's life.

The Beginners Guide to Homeschooling by Farenga, Patrick
Published by: Holt Associates, 2000, ISBN 0-916377-17-5
Contains questions and in-depth answers about homeschooling, suggestions for creating or purchasing curricula, thoughts on record keeping and evaluation and more.

Dumbing Us Down; The Hidden Curriculum of Compulsory Schooling by Gatto, John Taylor, Published by: New Society Publishing, 1991, ISBN 086571231X
This book was a revelation on how the compulsory school system works. Most people think that our schools aren't working. John Taylor Gatto outlines very clearly why the system is working—doing exactly what it was designed to do—indoctrinate our children.

The Unschooling Handbook; How to Use the Whole World As Your Child's Classroom by Griffith, Mary, Published by: Prima Publishing, 1998, ISBN 0761512764
Unschooling, defined by Griffith, as being founded on the principle that children learn best when they pursue their own natural curiosities and interests, is a term that means lots of things to lots of people. However, Griffith sticks to her definition and is able to describe how parents and children work together to create learning that is meaningful and lasting.

Family Matters; Why Homeschooling Makes Sense by Guterson, David
Published by: Harvest Books, 1993, ISBN 0156300001
Written by a public school teacher who is also a homeschool dad. He talks about how diversity in methods and curriculum are needed, yet not offered often by our schools. This book comes across as very philosophical, raises questions about money and democracy, and life before schools were the norm.

How Children Learn by Holt, John Caldwell
Published by: Perseus Press, 1995, ISBN 0201484048
Holt is a master at examining young children and understanding how their minds work. This loving and insightful look at the way children learn challenges and traditional assumptions, underlies all of Holt's later thinking, including his support for homeschooling.

What do I do on Monday? by Holt, John
Published by: Heinemann, 1995, ISBN 0867093684
This is Holt's classic answer to teachers who asked, "How can I put all your ideas into practice?" The book contains hundreds of things to do or try like measuring speed, measuring strength, fractions, recording talk, writing for ourselves, writing for others and much more. It also takes a hard look at what's wrong with marking and grading, at what can help troubled children, and the difference between "teacher as cop" and "teacher as guide." Holt wrote that of all his books, he felt that this was the one homeschoolers would find most practical.

Learning All the Time by Holt, John Caldwell
Published by: Perseus Press, 1990, ISBN 0201550911
John Holt was working on this book before his death and it was completed using his articles in *Growing without Schooling* and other previously uncollected writing. It demonstrates that children, without being coerced or manipulated and can pick up the basics from the world around them.

John suggests simple ways anyone can give children the slight assistance they may need to learn reading, writing, math, science and music.

Punished By Rewards, the Problems with Gold Stars, Incentive Plans, A's, Praise and Other Bribes by Kohn, Alfie
Published by: Houghton Mifflin Co., 1999, ISBN 0618001816
Punished by Rewards is probably the best book available concerning motivation, learning and living. The book is logical, well written and very enlightening. Motivation and intrinsic value belong to people, using artificial rewards (and punishment) is the best way to keep kids and adults from truly loving to learn and work. Rewards shift the focus from doing for personal value to working toward an external reward. This books is a real eye opener.

Raising Your Spirited Child by Kurcinka, Mary Sheedy
Published by: Harpercollins, 1992, ISBN 0060923288
This book gives parents of spirited (often called strong willed or difficult) children hope and with practical tips on how to enjoy and deal with your child. Extremely valuable for those struggling with their child's strong will.

Freedom Challenge Edited by Llewllyn, Grace
Published by: Lowry House Publishing, 1996 , ISBN 0962959111
This book features essays by, and interviews with, 16 children, teenagers, mothers and fathers. There is an important discussion about homeschooling as a continuation of the Civil Rights movement. It also wonderful material on young children teaching themselves to read, on setting up classes and networks for homeschoolers, and on how to homeschool with little money or as a single-parent.

Real Lives; Eleven Teenagers Who Don't Go to School by Llewellyn, Grace (Editor)
Published by: Lowry House Publishing, 1993, ISBN 0962959138

This is a wonderful book of essays by unschooled teens. The teens share their thoughts on unschooling, their lives and their own unique passions. This book shows just how diverse people are when allowed to follow their own interests.

The Teenage Liberation Handbook; How to Quit School and Get a Real Life and Education by Llewellyn, Grace
Published by: Lowry House Publishing, 1998, ISBN 1862041040
This book is written primarily for teens to show them that not only can they teach themselves, but truly can get a better education. It is also an awesome reassurance to parents as she has chapter upon chapter outlining exactly what's available out there for your children to learn. Great resources and ideas.

Homeschooling on a Shoestring; A Jam-packed Guide by Morgan, Melissa L., Allee, Judith Waite, McCoy, Jonni
Published by: Harold Shaw Publishers., 1999, ISBN 087788546
If you are looking to save money on either homeschooling or running your home, this is the book to get. The authors have spent considerable time putting together some of the best money saving tips available. Easy to navigate and very reader friendly.

A Sense of Self : Listening to Homeschooled Adolescent Girls by Sheffer, Susannah
Published by: Heinemann, 1997, ISBN 0867094052
Susannah Sheffer interviews 55 adolescent girls who are homeschooled. Their sense of who they are and how they see themselves is wonderfully refreshing and encouraging to homeschoolers with daughters.

Senior High: A Home-Designed Form+u+la By Shelton, Barb
Published by: Homeschool Seminars and Publications 1999, ISBN 1887639098

For many parents, the tendency at the high school level, is, as one homeschool mom said, to "just buckle down, take the textbooks by the horns and just DO it!" She sadly added: "The joy went right out the window!" This book is oozing with inspiration and practical help for homeschooling through high school.

The Homeschool Jumpstart Navigator For Younger Children by Barb Shelton, Published by: Homeschool Seminars and Publications
ISBN 1887639055
Don't have a clue as to where to start? Burned out on "school at home?" For either case, this 90-page book is brimming with practical help to get your child (re-)started onto a plan of learning.

Magazines

Home Education Learning Magazine (HELM) - A bimonthly magazine focusing on independent learning and self-directed education. HELM's goal is to encourage people to think about education in new ways and to offer support and information to those who are involved in home education. For subscription Information Contact HELM, 4200 AL Highway 157, Danville, AL 35619. 256-974-3017. Web: www.helmonline.com.

Growing Without Schooling - GWS is an ongoing conversation among its readers. The topics cover every imaginable concern or question about homeschooling. GWS also offers news about the homeschooling movement in the U.S. and abroad, reviews useful books and materials, and helps you connect with others through a directory of families and organizations. For ordering information and catalog contact: John Holt's Bookstore 2380 Massachusetts Ave Suite 104, Cambridge, MA 02140-1226, phone (617) 864-3100. Web: www.holtgws.com.

Home Education Magazine - This is the most widely recommended publication available for homeschooling families. Each issue includes several feature articles, interviews with today's most interesting personalities, outstanding columnists writing about topics of interest to homeschooling families, in-depth news reports, letters from readers, reviews, resources, penpals, networking and much more! Call toll-free: 1-800-236-3278 or email HEM-Info@home-ed-magazine.com (be sure to include your name and address). Postal mailing address: Home Education Magazine Post Office Box 1083 Tonasket, WA 98855-1083.

Family Unschoolers Network - Home for Unschooling Support newsletter. 1688 Belhaven Woods Ct, Pasadena, MD 21122-3727, 888-386-7020 (orders only)

Gentle Spirit Magazine - This is a wonderful Christian magazine on simple and deliberate living. It frequently includes articles on Christian unschooling. www.Gentlespirit.com PO Box 246, Wauna, WA 98395

TEACH ("To Encourage And Challenge Homeschoolers") is a 28-page quarterly publication, where you will hear from some experienced "keepers of the home" and prominent homeschoolers. For a sample issue or subscription information, send $2 to: 18016 West Spring Lake Drive, Renton, WA 98058.

Other Champion Press, Ltd. Homeschooling Products…

A Charlotte Mason Education by Catherine Levison
More Charlotte Mason Education by Catherine Levison
A Literary Education by Catherine Levison
Healthy Foods: Unit Study Grades K-5 by Leanne Ely, C.N.C.
Healthy Foods: Unit Study Grades 6-9 by Leanne Ely, C.N.C.
History and Science (Audio) by Catherine Levison
Balancing Act: to structure or not to structure (Audio)
Language Arts for Almost Free (Audio) by Catherine Levison
An Overview of the Charlotte Mason Method by Catherine Levison

for information on all of our
resources and products, visit us online at

www.championpress.com